Grade 5

Comprehension and Critical Thinking

TIME FOR KIDS

✓ Test Preparation

✓ Comprehension and Critical Thinking Questions

✓ Document-Based Analysis

Author

Jamey Acosta

The articles in this book are collected from the TIME For Kids archives.

SHELL EDUCATION

Editors
Diana Herweck, Psy.D.
Jodene Lynn Smith, M.A.

Assistant Editors
Leslie Huber, M.A.
Katie Das

Editorial Director
Dona Herweck Rice

Editor-in-Chief
Sharon Coan, M.S.Ed.

Editorial Manager
Gisela Lee, M.A.

Creative Director
Lee Aucoin

Cover Designer
Lee Aucoin

Cover Image
Compilation from NASA

Illustration Manager
Timothy J. Bradley

Artist
Kelly Brownlee

Interior Layout Designer and Print Production
Don Tran

Publisher
Corinne Burton, M.A.Ed.

Standards Compendium, Copyright 2004 McREL

Shell Education

5301 Oceanus Drive
Huntington Beach, CA 92649
http://www.shelleducation.com
ISBN 978-1-4258-0245-5
© *2008 Shell Educational Publishing, Inc.*
Reprinted 2013

Table of Contents

Introduction

Introduction and Research

Comprehension is the primary goal of any reading task. According to the RAND Reading Study Group, comprehension is "the process of simultaneously extracting and constructing meaning through interaction and involvement with written language" (2002, 11). Students who comprehend what they read have more opportunities in life, as well as better test performance. In order for students to become proficient readers, it is necessary that they are taught comprehension strategies such as predicting, monitoring comprehension, summarizing, visualizing, questioning, making connections, and inferring meaning (Miller 2002; Pardo 2002).

Focus on reading comprehension has become more urgent in light of NCLB legislation and emphasis on standardized testing. Because the majority of text found on standardized tests is nonfiction (Grigg, Daane, Jin, & Campbell 2003), teachers are now finding a greater need to teach skills using informational texts. For this reason, *Comprehension and Critical Thinking* provides teachers with informational texts in the form of articles about the contemporary world, as well as the past.

Research suggests that students need preparation in order to be successful on standardized tests. Gulek states: "Adequate and appropriate test preparation plays an important role in helping students demonstrate their knowledge and skills in high-stakes testing situations" (2003, 42). This preparation includes, among other things, teaching content and test-taking skills. Skills practiced when using the articles in *Comprehension and Critical Thinking* provide an excellent foundation for improving students' test-taking abilities.

Not only is reading nonfiction texts beneficial for testing purposes, but studies also show that students actually prefer informational texts. A 1998 study by Kletzien that focused on children's preferences for reading material indicated that younger children chose nonfiction text close to half the time when choosing their own reading materials. Similar studies (Ivey & Broaddus 2000; Moss & Hendershot 2002) revealed that older children prefer nonfiction and find greater motivation when reading informational texts.

In this book, each nonfiction passage includes a document-based question similar to trends in standardized testing. The students respond to a critical-thinking question based on the information gleaned from a given document. This document is related to the passage it accompanies. Document-based questions show a student's ability to apply prior knowledge and his or her capacity to transfer knowledge to a new situation. The activities are time efficient, allowing students to practice these skills every week. To yield the best results, such practice must begin at the start of the school year.

Students will need to use test-taking skills and strategies throughout their lives. The exercises in *Comprehension and Critical Thinking* will guide your students to become better readers and test takers. After practicing the exercises in this book, you will be pleased with your students' comprehension performance not only on standardized tests, but also with any expository text they encounter within the classroom and beyond its walls.

Objectives

All lessons in this book are designed to support the following objectives.

The students will:

- answer who, what, where, why, when, and how questions about the article
- support answers with information found in the article
- support answers with information inferred from the article
- support answers with information based on prior knowledge
- identify the main ideas in the article
- identify supporting details in the article
- draw conclusions based on information learned in the article
- make predictions based on information learned in the article
- form and defend an opinion based on information learned in the article
- respond to questions in written form

Readability

All the reading passages included in this book have a 5.0–5.9 reading level based on the Flesch-Kincaid Readability Formula. This formula determines a readability level by calculating the number of words, syllables, and sentences.

Preparing Students to Read Nonfiction Text

One of the best ways to prepare students to read expository text is to read a short selection aloud daily. Reading expository text aloud is critical to developing your students' abilities to read it themselves. Because making predictions is another way to help students tap into their prior knowledge, read the beginning of a passage, then stop and ask the students to predict what might occur next. Do this at several points throughout your reading of the text. By doing this over time, you will find that your students' ability to make accurate predictions greatly increases.

Of course, talking about nonfiction concepts is also very important. However, remember that discussion can never replace actually reading nonfiction texts because people rarely speak using the vocabulary and complex sentence structures of written language.

Asking questions helps students, especially struggling readers, to focus on what is important in a text. Also, remember the significance of wait time. Research has shown that the amount of time an educator waits for a student to answer after posing a question has a critical effect on learning. So, after you ask a student a question, silently count to five (or 10, if you have a student who struggles to get his or her thoughts into words) before giving any additional prompts or redirecting the question to another student.

Bloom's Taxonomy

The questions that follow each passage in *Comprehension and Critical Thinking* assess all levels of learning by following Bloom's Taxonomy, a six-level classification system for comprehension questions that was devised by Benjamin Bloom in 1956. The questions that follow each passage are always presented in order, progressing from *knowledge* to *evaluation*.

The skills listed for each level are essential to keep in mind when teaching comprehension in order to assure that your students reach the higher levels of thinking. Use this classification to form your own questions whenever your students listen to or read material.

Level 1: Knowledge—Students recall information or find requested information in an article. They show memory of dates, events, places, people, and main ideas.

Level 2: Comprehension—Students understand information. This means that they can find information that is stated in a different way from how the question is presented. It also means that students can rephrase or restate information in their own words.

Level 3: Application—Students apply their knowledge to a specific situation. They may be asked to do something new with the knowledge.

Level 4: Analysis—Students break things into components and examine those parts. They notice patterns in information.

Level 5: Synthesis—Students do something new with the information. They pull knowledge together to create new ideas. They generalize, predict, plan, and draw conclusions.

Level 6: Evaluation—Students make judgments and assess value. They form opinions and defend them. They can also understand another person's viewpoint.

Practice Suggestions: Short-Answer Questions

The short-answer question for each passage is evaluative—the highest level of Bloom's Taxonomy. It is basically an opinion statement with no definitive right answer. The students are asked to take stances and defend them. While there is no correct response, it is critical to show the students how to support their opinions using facts and logic. Show the students a format for response—state their opinion followed by the word *because* and a reason. For example, "I do not think that whales should be kept at sea parks because they are wild animals and don't want to be there. They want to be in the ocean with their friends." Do not award credit unless the child adequately supports his or her conclusion. Before passing back the practice papers, make note of two children who had opposing opinions. Then, during the discussion, call on each of these students to read his or her short-answer response to the class. (If all the children drew the same conclusion, come up with support for the opposing one yourself.)

Practice Suggestions: Document-Based Questions

It is especially important to guide your students in how to understand, interpret, and respond to the document-based questions. For these questions, in order to formulate a response, the students will have to rely on their prior knowledge and common sense in addition to the information provided in the document. Again, the best way to teach this is to demonstrate through thinking aloud how to figure out an answer. Since these questions are usually interpretive, you can allow for some variation in student responses.

The more your students practice, the more competent and confident they will become. Plan to have the class do every exercise in *Comprehension and Critical Thinking.* If you have some students who cannot read the articles independently, allow them to read with partners, and then work through the comprehension questions alone. Eventually, all students must practice reading and answering the questions independently. Move to this stage as soon as possible. For the most effective practice sessions, follow these steps:

1. Have the students read the text silently and answer the questions.

2. Collect all the papers to score the short-answer question and the document-based question portions.

3. Return the papers to their owners, and discuss how the students determined their answers.

4. Refer to the exact wording in the passage.

5. Point out how students had to use their background knowledge to answer certain questions.

6. Discuss how a student should explain his or her stance in each short-answer question.

7. Discuss the document-based questions thoroughly.

Practice Suggestions: Document-Based Extension Activities

The document-based extension activities provide students with opportunities to investigate topics related to the article in more detail. It may be useful to complete several of the document-based extension activities as a whole class prior to assigning them for students to complete independently. By doing so, students will develop an understanding of how the activities relate to the article that was read, the types of activities that are available, as well as the amount of detail needed to successfully complete an activity.

The document-based extension activities can be completed individually, in pairs, or in small groups. You may assign the activities to the students, or allow the students to select an activity that interests them.

Scoring the Practice Passages

Identify the number of correct responses when scoring the practice passages. Share the number of correct responses with the students. This is the number they will most easily identify; additionally, the number of correct responses coincides with the Student Achievement Graph. However, for your own records and to share with the parents, you may want to keep track of numeric scores for each student. If you choose to do this, do not write the numeric score on the paper.

To generate a numeric score, follow this example:

Type of Question	Number of Questions	Points Possible Per Question	Total Number of Points
Short-answer questions	6	5 points each	30 points
Document-based questions	2	20 points	40 points
Document-based extension	1	30 points	30 points
Total			**100 points**

Standardized Test Success

One of the key objectives of *Comprehension and Critical Thinking* is to prepare your students to get the best possible scores on the reading portion of standardized tests. A student's ability to do well on traditional standardized tests in comprehension requires these factors:

- a large vocabulary
- test-taking skills
- the ability to effectively cope with stress

Every student in your class needs instruction in test-taking skills. Even fluent readers and logical thinkers will perform better on standardized tests if you provide instruction in the following areas:

Understanding the question—Teach the students how to break down the question to figure out what is really being asked. This book will prepare the students for the kinds of questions they will encounter on standardized tests.

Concentrating only on what the text says—Show the students how to restrict their responses to only what is asked. When you review the practice passages, ask your students to show where they found the correct response in the text.

Ruling out distracters in multiple-choice answers—Teach the students to look for the key words in a question and look for those specific words to find the information in the text. They also need to know that they may have to look for synonyms for the key words.

Maintaining concentration—Use classroom time to practice this in advance. Reward the students for maintaining concentration. Explain to them the purpose of this practice and the reason why concentration is so essential.

Teaching Nonfiction Comprehension Skills

Nonfiction comprehension encompasses many skills that develop with a lot of practice. The following information offers a brief overview of the crucial skills of recognizing text structure, visualizing, summarizing, and learning new vocabulary. This information is designed for use with other classroom materials, not the practice passages in *Comprehension and Critical Thinking*.

Many of these skills can be found in scope-and-sequence charts and standards for reading comprehension:

- recognizes the main idea
- identifies details
- determines sequence
- recalls details
- labels parts
- summarizes
- identifies time sequence
- describes character(s)
- retells information in own words

- classifies, sorts into categories
- compares and contrasts
- makes generalizations
- draws conclusions
- recognizes text organization
- predicts outcome and consequences
- experiences an emotional reaction to a text
- recognizes facts
- applies information to a new situation

Typical Comprehension Questions

Teaching the typical kinds of standardized-test questions gives students an anticipation framework and helps them learn how to comprehend what they read. It also boosts their test scores. Questions generally found on standardized reading comprehension tests are as follows:

Facts—questions based on what the text states: who, what, when, where, why, and how

Sequence—questions based on order: what happened first, last, and in-between

Conditions—questions asking the students to compare, contrast, and find the similarities and differences

Summarizing—questions that require the students to restate, paraphrase, choose main ideas, conclude, and select a title

Vocabulary—questions based on word meaning, synonyms and antonyms, proper nouns, words in context, technical words, geographical words, and unusual adjectives

Outcomes—questions that ask readers to draw upon their own experiences or prior knowledge, which means that students must understand cause and effect, consequences, and implications

Opinion—questions that ask the author's intent and require the use of inference skills

Document based—questions that require students to analyze information from a source document to draw a conclusion or form an opinion

Teaching Text Structure

Students lacking in knowledge of text structure are at a distinct disadvantage, yet this skill is sometimes overlooked in instruction. When referring to a text to locate information to answer a question, understanding structure allows students to quickly locate the right area in which to look. The students also need to understand text structure in order to make predictions and improve overall comprehension.

Some students have been so immersed in print that they have a natural understanding of structure. For instance, they realize that the first sentence of a paragraph often contains the main idea, followed by details about that idea. But many students need direct instruction in text structure. The first step in this process is making certain that students know the way that authors typically present ideas in writing. This knowledge is a major asset for students.

Transitional paragraphs join together two paragraphs to make the writing flow. Most transitional paragraphs do not have a main idea. In all other paragraph types, there is a main idea, even if it is not stated. In the following examples, the main idea is italicized. In order of frequency, the four types of expository paragraph structures are as follows:

1. **The main idea is often the first sentence of a paragraph. The rest of the paragraph provides the supporting details.**

   Clara Barton, known as America's first nurse, was a brave and devoted humanitarian. While caring for others, she was shot at, got frostbitten fingers, and burned her hands. She had severe laryngitis twice and almost lost her eyesight. Yet she continued to care for the sick and injured until she died at the age of 91.

2. **The main idea may fall in the center of the paragraph, surrounded on both sides by details.**

   The coral has created a reef where more than 200 kinds of birds and about 1,500 types of fish live. *In fact, Australia's Great Barrier Reef provides a home for many interesting animals.* These include sea turtles, giant clams, crabs, and crown-of-thorns starfish.

3. **The main idea comes at the end of the paragraph as a summary of the details that came before.**

   Each year, Antarctica spends six months in darkness, from mid-March to mid-September. The continent is covered year-round by ice, which causes sunlight to reflect off its surface. It never really warms up. In fact, the coldest temperature ever recorded was in Antarctica. *Antarctica has one of the harshest environments in the world.*

4. **The main idea is not stated in the paragraph and must be inferred from the details given. This paragraph structure is the most challenging for primary students.**

   The biggest sea horse ever found was over a foot long. Large sea horses live along the coasts of New Zealand, Australia, and California. Smaller sea horses live off the coast of Florida, in the Caribbean Sea, and in the Gulf of Mexico. The smallest adult sea horse ever found was only one-half inch long!

   In this example, the implied main idea is that sea horses' sizes vary based on where they live.

Teaching Text Structure *(cont.)*

Some other activities that will help your students understand text structure include the following:

Color code—While reading a text, have the students use different-colored pencils or highlighters to color-code important elements such as the main idea (red), supporting details (yellow), causes (green) and effects (purple), and facts (blue) and opinions (orange). When they have finished, ask them to describe the paragraph's structure in their own words.

Search the text—Teach the students to identify the key words in a question and look specifically for those words in the passage. Then, when you discuss a comprehension question with the students, ask them, "Which words will you look for in the text to find the answer? If you can't find the words, can you find synonyms? Where will you look for the words?"

Signal words—There are specific words used in text that indicate, or signal, that the text has a cause-effect, sequence, or comparison structure. Teaching your students these words will greatly improve their abilities to detect text structure and increase their comprehension.

These Signal Words ...	Indicate ...
since, because, caused by, as a result, before and after, so, this led to, if/then, reasons, brought about, so that, when/then, that's why	cause and effect The answer to "Why did it happen?" is a cause. The answer to "What happened?" is an effect.
first, second, third, next, then, after, before, last, later, since then, now, while, meanwhile, at the same time, finally, when, at last, in the end, since that time, following, on (date), at (time)	sequence
but, even if, even though, although, however, instead, not only, unless, yet, on the other hand, either/or, as well as, "–er" and "–st" words (such as better, best, shorter, tallest, bigger, smallest, most, worst)	compare/contrast

Teaching Visualization Skills

Visualization—Visualization is seeing the words of a text as mental images. It is a significant factor that sets proficient readers apart from low-achieving ones. Studies have shown that the ability to generate vivid images while reading strongly correlates with a person's comprehension of text. However, research has also revealed that 20 percent of all children do not visualize or experience sensory images when reading. These children are thus handicapped in their ability to comprehend text, and they are usually the students who avoid and dislike reading because they never connect to text in a personal, meaningful way.

Active visualization can completely engross a reader in text. You have experienced this when you just could not put a book down and you stayed up all night just to finish it. Skilled readers automatically weave their own memories into text as they read to make personalized, lifelike images. In fact, every person develops a unique interpretation of any text. This personalized reading experience explains why most people prefer a book to its movie.

Visualization is not static; unlike photographs, these are "movies in the mind." Mental images must constantly be modified to incorporate new information as it is disclosed by the text. Therefore, your students must learn how to revise their images if they encounter information that requires them to do so.

Sensory Imaging—Sensory imaging employs other senses besides sight, and is closely related to visual imaging. It too has been shown to be crucial to the construction of meaning during reading. This is because the more senses that are employed in a task, the more neural pathways are built, resulting in more avenues to access information. You have experienced sensory imaging when you could almost smell the smoke of a forest fire or taste the sizzling bacon, or laughed along with a character as you read. Sensory imaging connects the reader personally and intimately to the text and breathes life into words.

Since visualization is a challenging skill for one out of every five students to develop, begin with simple fictional passages to scaffold their attempts and promote success. After your students have experienced success with visualization and sensory imaging in literature, they are ready to employ these techniques in nonfiction text.

Visualization has a special significance in nonfiction text. The technical presentation of ideas in nonfiction text coupled with new terms and concepts often overwhelm and discourage students. Using visualization can help students move beyond these barriers. As an added benefit, people who create mental images display better long-term retention of factual material.

Clearly, there are important reasons to teach visualization and sensory imaging skills to students. But perhaps the most compelling reason is this: visualizing demands active involvement, turning passive students into active constructors of meaning.

Teaching Visualization Skills *(cont.)*

Doing Think-Alouds—It is essential for you to introduce visualization by doing think-alouds to describe your own visualization of text. To do this, read aloud the first one or two lines of a passage and describe what images come to your mind. Be sure to include details that were not stated in the text, such as the house has two stories and green shutters. Then, read the next two lines, and explain how you add to or modify your image based on the new information provided by the text. When you are doing a think-aloud for your class, be sure to do the following:

- Explain how your images help you to better understand the passage.
- Describe details, being sure to include some from your own schema.
- Mention the use of your senses—the more the better.
- Describe your revision of the images as you read further and encounter new information.

Teaching Summarizing

Summarizing informational text is a crucial skill for students to master. It is also one of the most challenging. Summarizing means pulling out only the essential elements of a passage—just the main idea and supporting details. Research has shown that having students put information into their own words causes it to be processed more thoroughly. Thus, summarizing increases both understanding and long-term retention of material. Information can be summarized through such diverse activities as speaking, writing, drawing, or creating a project.

The basic steps of summarizing are as follows:

- Look for the paragraph's main idea sentence; if there is none, create one.
- Find the supporting details, being certain to group all related terms or ideas.
- Record information that is repeated or restated only once.
- Put the summary together into an organized format.

Scaffolding is of critical importance. Your students will need a lot of modeling, guided practice, and small-group or partner practice before attempting to summarize independently. All strategies should be done as a whole group and then with a partner several times before letting the students practice them on their own. Encourage the greatest transfer of knowledge by modeling each strategy's use in multiple content areas.

Teaching Vocabulary

Students may see a word in print that they have never read or heard before. As a result, students need direct instruction in vocabulary to make real progress toward becoming readers who can independently access expository text. Teaching the vocabulary that occurs in a text significantly improves comprehension. Because students encounter vocabulary terms in science, social studies, math, and language arts, strategies for decoding and understanding new words must be taught throughout the day.

Students' vocabularies develop in this order: listening, speaking, reading, and writing. This means that a child understands a word when it is spoken to him or her long before using it in speech. The child will also understand the word when reading it before attempting to use it in writing. Each time a child comes across the same word, understanding of that word deepens. Research has shown that vocabulary instruction has the most positive effect on reading comprehension when students encounter the words multiple times. That is why the best vocabulary instruction requires students to use new words in writing and speaking as well as in reading.

Teaching vocabulary can be both effective and fun, especially if you engage the students' multiple modalities (listening, speaking, reading, and writing). In addition, instruction that uses all four modalities is most apt to reach every learner.

The more experience a child has with language, the stronger his or her vocabulary base. Therefore, the majority of vocabulary activities should be done as whole-group or small-group instruction. In this way, children with limited vocabularies can learn from their peers' knowledge bases and will find vocabulary activities less frustrating. Remember, too, that a picture is worth a thousand words. Whenever possible, provide pictures of new vocabulary words.

Selecting Vocabulary Words to Study

Many teachers feel overwhelmed when teaching vocabulary because they realize that it is impossible to thoroughly cover all the words students may not know. Do not attempt to study every unknown word. Instead, wisely choose the words from each selection. Following these guidelines in order will result in an educationally sound vocabulary list:

- Choose words that are critical to the article's meaning.
- Choose conceptually difficult words.
- Choose words with the greatest utility value—those that you anticipate the children will see more often (e.g., choose *horrified* rather than *appalled*).

These suggestions are given for teaching nonfiction material in general. Do not select and preteach vocabulary from these practice passages. You want to simulate real test conditions in which the children would have no prior knowledge of any of the material in any of the passages.

Teaching Vocabulary (cont.)

Elements of Effective Vocabulary Instruction

Vocabulary instruction is only effective if students permanently add the concepts to their knowledge bases. Research has shown that the most effective vocabulary program includes contextual, structural, and classification strategies. You can do this by making certain that your vocabulary instruction includes the following elements:

- using context clues
- knowing the meaning of affixes (prefixes, suffixes) and roots
- introducing new words as synonyms and antonyms of known words

Using Context Clues

Learning vocabulary in context is important for two reasons. First, it allows students to become active in determining word meanings; and second, it transfers into their lives by offering them a way to figure out unknown words in their independent reading. If you teach your students how to use context clues, you may eventually be able to omit preteaching any vocabulary that is defined in context (so long as the text is written at your students' independent levels).

There are five basic kinds of context clues.

- **Definition**—The definition is given elsewhere in the sentence or paragraph.

  Example: The ragged, *tattered* dress hung from her shoulders.

- **Synonym**—A synonym or synonymous phrase is immediately used in the sentence.

  Example: Although she was overweight, her *obesity* never bothered her until she went to middle school.

- **Contrast**—The meaning may be implied through contrast to a known word or concept. Be alert to these words that signal contrast: *although, but, however,* and *even though.*

  Example: Although Adesha had always been *prompt*, today he was 20 minutes late.

- **Summary**—The meaning is summed up by a list of attributes.

  Example: Tundra, desert, grassland, and rain forest are four of Earth's *biomes.*

- **Mood**—The meaning of the word can sometimes be grasped from the mood of the larger context in which it appears. The most difficult situation is when the meaning must be inferred with few other clues.

  Example: Her *shrill* voice was actually making my ears hurt.

Building Vocabulary

Your general approach to building vocabulary should include the following:

Brainstorming—Students brainstorm a list of words associated with a familiar word, sharing everyone's knowledge and thoroughly discussing unfamiliar words.

Semantic mapping—Students sort the brainstormed words into categories, often creating a visual organization tool—such as a graphic organizer or word web—to depict the relationships.

Feature analysis—Students are provided with the key features of the text and a list of terms in a chart, such as a semantic matrix or Venn diagram. Have the students identify the similarities and differences between the items.

Synonyms and antonyms—Introduce both synonyms and antonyms for the words to provide a structure for meaning and substantially and rapidly increase your students' vocabularies.

Analogies—Analogies are similar to synonyms but require higher-level thinking. The goal is to help students identify the relationship between words. Analogies appear on standardized tests in the upper elementary grades.

> **Example:** Bark is to tree as skin is to <u>human</u>.

Word affixes—Studying common prefixes and suffixes helps students deduce new words, especially in context. Teach students to ask, "Does this look like any other word I know? Can I find any word parts I know? Can I figure out the meaning based on its context?"

Important Affixes for Primary Grades

Prefix	Meaning	Example	Suffix	Meaning	Example
un	not	unusual	**-s or -es**	more than one	cars; tomatoes
re	again	redo	**-ed**	did an action	moved
in, im	not	impassable	**-ing**	doing an action	buying
dis	opposite	disassemble	**-ly**	like, very	usually
non	not	nonathletic	**-er**	a person who	farmer
over	too much	overcook	**-ful**	full of	respectful
mis	bad	misrepresent	**-or**	a person who	creator
pre	before	prearrange	**-less**	without	harmless
de	opposite	decompose	**-er**	more	calmer
under	less	underachieve	**-est**	most	happiest

Correlation to Standards

The No Child Left Behind (NCLB) legislation mandates that all states adopt academic standards that identify the skills students will learn in kindergarten through grade 12. While many states had already adopted academic standards prior to NCLB, the legislation set requirements to ensure the standards were detailed and comprehensive.

Standards are designed to focus instruction and guide adoption of curricula. Standards are statements that describe the criteria necessary for students to meet specific academic goals. They define the knowledge, skills, and content students should acquire at each level. Standards are also used to develop standardized tests to evaluate students' academic progress.

In many states today, teachers are required to demonstrate how their lessons meet state standards. State standards are used in the development of Shell Education products, so educators can be assured that they meet the academic requirements of each state.

How to Find Your State Correlations

Shell Education is committed to producing educational materials that are research and standards based. In this effort, all products are correlated to the academic standards of the 50 states, the District of Columbia, and the Department of Defense Dependent Schools. A correlation report customized for your state can be printed directly from the following website: **http://www.shelleducation.com**. If you require assistance in printing correlation reports, please contact Customer Service at 1-877-777-3450.

McREL Compendium

Shell Education uses the Mid-continent Research for Education and Learning (McREL) Compendium to create standards correlations. Each year, McREL analyzes state standards and revises the compendium. By following this procedure, they are able to produce a general compilation of national standards.

Each reading comprehension strategy assessed in this book is based on one or more McREL content standards. The chart below shows the McREL standards that correlate to each lesson used in the book. To see a state-specific correlation, visit the Shell Education website at **http://www.shelleducation.com**.

Language Arts Standards

Standard 1   **Uses the general skills and strategies of the writing process.**

    1.2   Uses strategies to draft and revise written work.

Standard 5   **Uses the general skills and strategies of the reading process.**

    5.1   Uses mental images based on pictures and print to aid in comprehension of text.

    5.2   Uses meaning clues to aid comprehension.

Standard 7   **Uses reading skills and strategies to understand and interpret a variety of informational texts.**

    7.1   Uses reading skills and strategies to understand a variety of informational texts.

    7.2   Understands the main idea and supporting details of simple expository information.

    7.3   Summarizes information found in texts.

    7.4   Relates new information to prior knowledge and experiences.

Earth Day Heroes

He Has a Bright Idea

Avery Hairston is lighting up people's lives. The 15-year-old from New York City created a charity called RelightNY. It helps people who struggle to pay their energy bills by giving them compact fluorescent light bulbs, which reduce long-term energy costs. They are also better for the environment than regular bulbs. "People who can afford the bulbs, which are a bit expensive, should buy them for themselves and supply them to others," Avery insists.

He Is Big on Recycling

Eli Kahn, 15, started Cartridges for a Cure to raise money for children's cancer research by recycling empty ink cartridges. Eli has raised $82,000 for Johns Hopkins Children's Center. "With a little time and effort, anything can get bigger," Eli says.

She Makes Water Safe to Drink

Kelydra Welcker, 17, is on a mission to make drinking water safer. She invented an easy way to remove the chemical C8 from her West Virginia town's water supply. C8 seeped into the water from a nearby industrial plant. "Clean water should be a given," Kelydra explains. "Everyone should have it."

She Combats Deforestation

Wangari Maathai, from Kenya, Africa, has been working for 30 years to save the environment. In 1977, she started a movement in Kenya to help combat deforestation. The program has planted more than 30 million trees in Africa. Her work earned her the Nobel Peace Prize in 2004.

Now Maathai has invited the world to join her growing efforts. Last fall, she helped launch the Billion Tree Campaign. The United Nations program encourages people to plant trees in their communities, with the goal of planting one billion trees worldwide this year. Pledges to grow green have poured in, and more than nine million trees have been planted. Says Maathai, "This is something anybody can do."

Earth Day Heroes (cont.)

Directions: Answer the questions. You may use the article.

1. What is RelightNY? Who created it?

   _____

   _____

   _____

2. Summarize Kelydra Welcker's mission. What happened? What did she do? How did she do it? Explain the impact of her mission on those around her.

   _____

   _____

   _____

3. Why do you think Wangari Maathai won the Nobel Peace Prize? Describe how her movement has changed the world.

   _____

   _____

   _____

4. Compose a fictional letter to your local representative requesting assistance in organizing a community tree-planting day. Remember, you are trying to organize a community event; therefore the goal of this letter should be to acquire all the information necessary to do so. Use the back of this page for your letter.

5. In your own words, describe how the people mentioned in this article are alike. What kind of people are they? Do they share a similar view of the world?

   _____

   _____

   _____

6. Is it possible for one person to make a difference? What is it about the people celebrated in the article that leads you to believe one person can or cannot make a difference?

   _____

   _____

   _____

Earth Day Heroes *(cont.)*

What Can We Do?

In today's world, we have the opportunity to make choices that will impact our environment. Do you recycle? Do you conserve water? Do you help plant trees? Do you turn off the lights when you leave the room? Is your home as energy efficient as it could be? If you answered "no" to any of these questions, you are not alone! Many of us do not do enough to protect our environment. Maybe this is because we don't know where to start.

Did you know that if every household replaced just three 60-watt incandescent lightbulbs with compact fluorescent lightbulbs (CFLs), we would reduce as much pollution as if we took 3.5 million cars off the roads? That's just one example of how we can make a big difference.

Use the table provided to compare the two types of bulbs. Then answer the questions below.

Incandescent Lightbulb	Compact Fluorescent Lightbulb (CFL)
75 watt bulb used 6 hours/day = $12/year to operate	18 watt bulb used 6 hours/day = $3/year to operate
Less expensive to purchase	More expensive to purchase
Only 5–20 percent of energy used is converted to light; the rest is converted to heat	Uses up to $\frac{2}{3}$ less energy

1. Which type of bulb is the most energy efficient as well as the most cost effective over time?

   _____

   _____

2. What are the benefits of a CFL bulb compared to an incandescent bulb?

   _____

   _____

3. According to the chart above, how much money can a consumer save each year on operational costs by switching one bulb in his or her house to a CFL bulb? How much would the person save per year if he or she switched to 10 CFL bulbs?

   _____

   _____

   _____

   _____

Earth Day Heroes *(cont.)*

Document-Based Extension Activities

Students may work independently, or the teacher may copy this page and cut out the activities and distribute them to the students for completion in small groups.

1. Make a list of three ways your class can work together to protect the environment. Then pick one and come up with a plan to make it happen. Prepare a presentation to share with the rest of class.

2. Create a pledge for your classmates to agree to. For example, urge them to replace at least one incandescent light bulb to a CFL bulb. If necessary, ask for others to donate extra CFL bulbs to those in need.

3. Interview teachers and other school employees to see what they do with their old ink cartridges. Do they recycle them? Do they donate them? If they are throwing them away, tell them how they can recycle them.

4. Write a letter to your city water department. Ask about your city's water supply. Is it safe to drink? What measures are being used to ensure that it remains safe to drink? Is there anything you can do to help your city?

Population Boom!

The United States reached a big milestone on October 17, 2006. According to the United States Census Bureau's population clock, at 7:46 A.M., the number of people in the country hit 300 million. The clock uses an estimation formula that ticks off a birth every seven seconds, a death every 13 seconds, and the addition of a new immigrant every 31 seconds. That equals one new American every 11 seconds.

Calculating the number of people in a large country is not an easy job. The Census Bureau counts the nation's population every 10 years. The last official census, taken in 2000, was conducted by mail, by telephone, and through in-person interviews. That tally was 281,421,906 people. Since then, the Census Bureau has used the population clock to predict growth.

My, How We've Grown

By any measure, the United States population has exploded in recent years. It is the third most populous country in the world, behind China and India, each of which has a population of more than 1 billion. The United State's first census, taken in 1790, registered 3.9 million people. It took until 1915 for the tally to reach 100 million. When the population hit 200 million in 1967, President Lyndon B. Johnson held a press conference to celebrate.

Americans will likely number 400 million in 2043. Many things could affect this estimate, including new immigration policies. If current trends keep up, the United States will continue to become more diverse. White, non-Hispanic people will still be the majority, at about 52 percent. About 22 percent of the population will be Hispanic. People of many races consider themselves Hispanic. African Americans will make up 14 percent of the population and Asians 7 percent. The United States population is expected to grow by about 1 percent each year. That's about the same as the growth rate for the entire world. There are 6.5 billion people on the planet.

Some people did not cheer the new United States milestone. They worry about the population boom. "Americans will be using so much more of our share of the world's resources and kicking so much more pollution into the air," said Charles Westoff, a population expert.

Of today's Americans, 34.3 million were born in a foreign country. That's 12 percent of the total population. Experts predict that this number will keep climbing, making the country more diverse.

Name _____

Population Boom! (cont.)

Directions: Answer the questions. You may look at the article.

1. How often does the Census Bureau count the nation's population? When was the last census taken? When will the next census be conducted?

   _____

   _____

2. List the three most populous countries in the world in order.

   _____

3. In what year did the United States complete its first census? What were the results? Describe the growth that occurred from the year of the first census until 1967.

   _____

   _____

4. In October 2006, the United States population reached 300 million. Many people cheered and considered reaching that number a milestone. Other people, however, did not. Explain the feelings and fears of those who worry about this population boom.

   _____

   _____

   _____

5. What is the population estimate for Americans in 2043? How do you feel about that number? Do you have any concerns about our rapid population growth? Explain how the increase could affect you and your family.

   _____

   _____

   _____

6. Create a news article that describes your opinion on how the rise in population could affect our environment. Use the back of this page. You may need to research current environmental issues and concerns. **Hint:** Reread the quote by Charles Westoff in the second-to-last paragraph of the article.

Population Boom! (cont.)

300 Million and Counting
United States Population Milestones

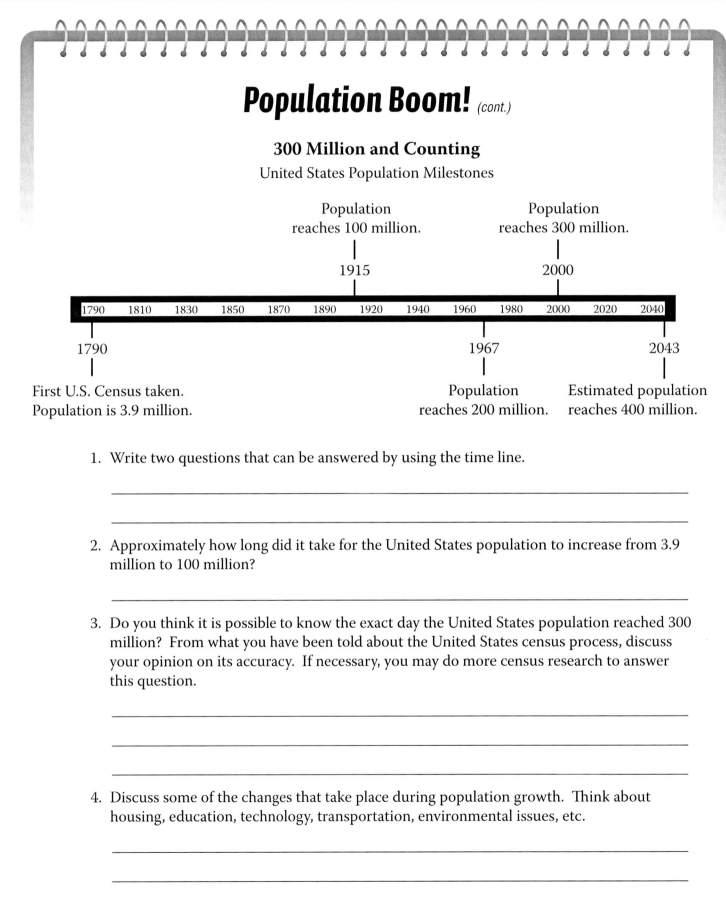

1. Write two questions that can be answered by using the time line.

   _____

   _____

2. Approximately how long did it take for the United States population to increase from 3.9 million to 100 million?

   _____

3. Do you think it is possible to know the exact day the United States population reached 300 million? From what you have been told about the United States census process, discuss your opinion on its accuracy. If necessary, you may do more census research to answer this question.

   _____

   _____

   _____

4. Discuss some of the changes that take place during population growth. Think about housing, education, technology, transportation, environmental issues, etc.

   _____

   _____

   _____

Population Boom! *(cont.)*

Document-Based Extension Activities

Students may work independently, or the teacher may copy this page and cut out the activities and distribute them to the students for completion in small groups.

1. We now know that China has a population that exceeds one billion. What do you think life is like in China? Imagine how our lives would be different with over a billion people living in the United States. Discuss the areas of your life you think would be the most affected by such a large population. Think of traffic, environmental concerns, housing, water supply, etc.

2. Think about population growth. Is growth always positive? What social, environmental, and economic effects can continued growth have on the United States? Create a brief presentation that discusses the potential problems you have identified.

3. Why do you think immigration policy and trends are such important factors in tracking and predicting population growth? How do we account for the number of illegal immigrants living in the United States? You may want to research this topic more on the Internet, or ask your social studies teacher to participate in your discussion.

4. What does the term *melting pot* mean to you? Explain why the United States is considered a melting pot. What does that mean? What are the benefits and risks associated with living in a melting pot?

It's Asthma Season

Jeremy Wirick, 9, recently had an asthma attack after he pushed himself too hard in gym class. When Jeremy got home an hour or two later, he was wheezing loudly. He needed to use a *nebulizer*, a machine that helps send medicine quickly to the lungs, to get his breathing back to normal. Asthma attacks like Jeremy's increase in September and October. More than six times as many asthma sufferers who are elementary-school age need hospital treatment in the fall as in the summer.

Experts believe many factors can contribute to back-to-school asthma. "When kids get together in close spaces, they start passing viruses around. A viral infection can trigger an asthma attack," said Dr. Norman Edelman, chief medical officer of the American Lung Association. "There are also certain fall allergies, such as molds and ragweed, that can trigger attacks." Exercise is another common cause of an attack. For some kids, the stress of school can make asthma worse.

Understanding Asthma

Asthma is a chronic, or long-term, disease that affects a person's airways, or breathing tubes. Humans breathe air through the nose or mouth into the windpipe. The air then travels through a network of narrow tubes to the lungs. During an asthma attack, the breathing tubes get narrower, which makes it harder for air to travel in and out of the lungs. As the tubes swell, they may produce extra mucus, which takes up space through which the air needs to travel.

The American Lung Association says that about 6.2 million American children suffer from asthma. That's about one out of 12 kids. Asthma is the chronic illness that causes students to miss the most days of school. But take a deep breath. There are many things that schools can do to help students control their asthma.

An Action Plan

Parents can play a big role in helping kids with asthma start the school year right. Before the school year starts, parents should notify school workers in writing about their son or daughter's asthma.

Kentucky and Delaware are two of the 47 states that have passed laws allowing students to carry their asthma medication with them at school. This gives the parents and the students the opportunity to decide whether or not to leave the inhaler in the nurse's office or to keep it on hand at all times.

It's Asthma Season (cont.)

Directions: Answer the questions. You may look at the article.

1. What is a nebulizer, and why is it important to someone with asthma?

    _____

    _____

2. What time of year do elementary school-aged children suffering from asthma have the most attacks? Explain some of the factors that contribute to the increase in asthma attacks during this time of year.

    _____

    _____

3. Which chronic illness causes students to miss the most school? Can you think of any steps schools can take to help reduce the amount of school days missed due to this illness?

    _____

    _____

4. Define asthma. Explain what happens during an asthma attack.

    _____

    _____

5. Imagine you are an asthma sufferer. Using the information presented in the article, determine how you would handle your condition at school. How would you feel around other students? Would you want your illness to be kept private? What about participating during P.E. or playing during recess? Describe how having asthma would impact your life.

    _____

    _____

    _____

6. Pretend you are a parent and write a letter to the school nurse explaining your child's condition. Include such information as when to take the medication, what to do in case of an attack, exercise restrictions, etc. Use the back of this paper to write your letter.

It's Asthma Season (cont.)

Read the sample letter to help you complete the questions below.

Dear School District,

I am a fifth-grade student who suffers from asthma. My asthma was so bad that I had to miss a lot of school last year. My parents and doctors were concerned about my health and my education. Together they came up with a solution—to begin reaching out to schools.

Do you know that there is something you can do to create a safe environment for your students? The National Heart, Lung, and Blood Institute says that you can take these simple steps to create a safe environment for kids.

- Provide good indoor air quality. The building should be free of dust, mold, and strong odors.
- Never allow smoking anywhere on school grounds or during any school-sponsored events.
- Review students' asthma action plans. The plan should be filled out by the student's doctor and should list what to do if the student's asthma gets worse at school. The school nurse should work with the student to help him or her follow the plan during the school day.
- Advise teachers to keep furry pets and other animals out of the classroom.
- Limit students' exposure to paint and chemicals in art and science class.
- Heavy cleaning and painting should be done after school hours.
- Instruct all teachers and students about asthma and how to help students who have it stay safe.

If you have missed anything on this list, please take action now—not only does the health of your students depend on your efforts, but their education does, too!

Sincerely,
Rebecca Aguilar

1. What is the purpose of this letter?

   _____

   _____

2. Do you feel that these steps are an important part of keeping your school environment safe? Explain your answer.

   _____

   _____

3. Predict how your school would react to this letter. What action(s) do you think they would take?

   _____

   _____

It's Asthma Season (cont.)

Document-Based Extension Activities

Students may work independently, or the teacher may copy this page and cut out the activities and distribute them to the students for completion in small groups.

1. Create a poster that illustrates different activities and conditions that may cause and/or prevent an asthma attack. For example: exercise, weather conditions, taking medication, etc.

2. Using the article and the sample letter to guide you, develop a brochure about kids and asthma. **Hint:** You may include the following sections—one section that introduces and explains the chronic illness, one section that describes conditions and activities that can be unsafe for asthma suffers, and one section that describes steps that you and your school can take to safely live with asthma.

3. Interview a student at your school who suffers from asthma. **Important:** Make sure the person you are interviewing is comfortable sharing this personal information with you. You may ask your own questions, or you may use some of the ones listed below.

   - How old were you when you first figured out you have asthma? How did this discovery make you feel?

   - Did you have to take a lot of tests at the doctor's office?

   - What is the hardest part about living with asthma?

   - What does it feel like when you are having an attack? Do you get scared?

4. What happens to one's body during an asthma attack? Discuss the possible causes and effects. Make two illustrations, one that shows the natural human breathing process and another one that demonstrates what happens to that process during an asthma attack.

Up in Smoke

Each April, Kick Butts Day, organized by the Campaign for Tobacco-Free Kids, draws attention to the deadly dangers of smoking. Young people across the country will wear T-shirts that say "1,200." That's the number of Americans who die every day from the effects of smoking and secondhand smoke. Such youth-led programs are just one strategy thought to be responsible for the drop in smoking in the United States.

Fighting Fire with Fire

Danny McGoldrick of the Campaign for Tobacco-Free Kids says the government has to get tougher if it wants to succeed. The campaign recommends three steps: Raising tobacco taxes, passing more smoke-free laws, and making sure that states spend additional money on antismoking programs.

In the late 1990s, all 50 states went to court to fight tobacco companies. The states won the cases and received big money from the cigarette makers. The money was to be used to pay for health care and fund antismoking campaigns. Combined with tobacco-tax earnings, the states now have $21.3 billion dollars for the antitobacco fight. But only $551 million is being spent on tobacco prevention. That may sound like a lot of money, but it's not when compared with the $15.1 billion the tobacco industry spends on advertising and sales.

Laws forbid cigarette companies from directly targeting young people, but there is no denying that kids are influenced by what they see. Magazine ads, store displays, Internet sales, and new products like sweet-flavored cigarettes all appeal to young tastes. When kids go to NASCAR races, music concerts, or the movies, they can't help but notice that their idols light up cigarettes. Recent research suggests that the more movies kids watch, the more likely they are to smoke. Each day, about 4,000 kids try cigarettes for the first time. Health experts say that they will keep fighting until all kids get the message that tobacco is deadly.

Blazing the Trail

Smoke-free environments and antismoking ads get the right message across. The American Legacy Foundation's Truth campaign exposes ugly facts about smoking and cigarette makers' tactics. Recently, Calabasas, California, added the toughest smoking law in the nation. It prohibits smoking in all public places, both indoors and outdoors.

Up in Smoke (cont.)

Directions: Answer the questions. You may look at the article.

1. What does the number 1,200 represent?

   _____

   _____

2. List the three steps the Campaign for Tobacco-Free Kids says the government must take to ensure that the smoking rates drop even further.

   _____

   _____

3. How many kids try cigarettes for the first time each day? Describe how that number makes you feel.

   _____

   _____

4. Summarize what happened to the money the states won fighting the tobacco companies in the late 1990s.

   _____

   _____

5. Compare the amount of money spent on tobacco prevention to the amount of money the tobacco industry spends on advertising and sales. Explain why this is a problem.

   _____

   _____

6. Describe how the media, Internet, movies, and celebrity idols can make smoking appealing to kids and teens.

   _____

   _____

7. Do you think the government should ban smoking in movies and TV shows aimed at kids and teens? Why or why not?

   _____

   _____

Up in Smoke (cont.)

Fighting Fire with Fire

Did you know that children with the highest exposure to smoking in movies are three times more likely to try smoking than those with less exposure? Did you know that smoking just one cigarette exposes a smoker and the air to more than 4,000 chemicals? Use the information provided to help you answer these questions and the ones below.

Current R Rating  R Rating due to tobacco use

1. Do you think all movies with tobacco use should be required to have an R rating? Why or why not?

_____

_____

_____

_____

2. If the R rating were required to include all movies with tobacco use, but parents were to allow their kids to see R-rated movies anyway, how would that affect the potential results of the new requirement?

_____

_____

_____

_____

3. Predict what might happen if kids and teens saw fewer movies with smoking in them.

_____

_____

_____

_____

Up in Smoke (cont.)

Document-Based Extension Activities

Students may work independently, or the teacher may copy this page and cut out the activities and distribute them to the students for completion in small groups.

1. Write and perform a skit that practices saying "no" to smoking cigarettes.

2. Write a letter to your local Congress member asking them to help spread the anti-smoking message to kids and teens. **Note:** You may also write to a specific organization or tobacco company if you prefer.

3. Find five tobacco advertisements and analyze them. Discuss how the tobacco companies use advertising to sell cigarettes and determine whom they are targeting in each advertisement. You may use magazines, Internet, movie clips, etc.

4. Develop an antismoking campaign for your school. **Hint:** You may want to consider the following ideas: come up with a catchy slogan for your campaign; create a contract for parents to sign that holds them accountable for monitoring their child's smoking exposure through the media; have the students at your school take a pledge that they will not smoke cigarettes; and/or organize an assembly that shares what you learned with the rest of your school. You may need to do additional research.

Attack of the Locusts

An angry army of hungry bugs have invaded, bringing big problems to much of northern Africa. Millions of locusts have invaded the region. The bugs gobble crops and destroy pastures. They leave little behind for other animals to eat.

The current wave of swarming insects is thought to be the biggest to attack Africa since 1988. "It's beautiful to see the locusts on parade in the sky," said Aicha Bint Sadibouh, who lives in Mauritania. "But when they invade streets and homes, it's disastrous."

Fighting a Nasty Nuisance

A locust starts life as a wingless insect the size of a large ant. Adult locusts develop wings. Alone, a locust can't cause much damage. But when they swarm, the bugs become more aggressive. When millions of locusts invade a region, they devour every plant in sight and then move on. A swarm can destroy more than 120 miles in a single day. "Some farmers are afraid to plant any more seeds," says Keith Cressman of the United Nations Food and Agriculture Organization. "They're afraid (the seeds) will be attacked by the locusts."

Locust groups lay thousands of eggs, creating new generations of hungry bugs every three months. If enough bugs are born this year and spread across several countries, the result could be tragic. Many Africans would likely die of starvation as a result of the invading bugs eating their food and crops.

The United Nations is coordinating efforts to help the affected countries. The plan is to spray pesticides on as many fields as possible throughout the region. Last summer, Algeria, Morocco, and Tunisia successfully sprayed fields, controlling a major locust invasion.

So far, locusts have spread through Sudan, Chad, Niger, Mali, Senegal, and Mauritania. These countries are poor, but they're fighting back. In Mali, President Amadou Toumani Toure and members of his government donated a month's salary to help pay for the battle against the bugs. In Senegal, people who bring in 11 pounds of dead locusts are rewarded with 110 pounds of rice. Said Senegal's president, Abdoulaye Wade: "For me, this is a real war."

Attack of the Locusts *(cont.)*

Directions: Answer the questions. You may use the article.

1. What is a locust? What is the difference between a single locust and a swarm of locusts?

    _____

    _____

2. Describe what happens to crops and pastures when a swarm of locusts hits.

    _____

    _____

3. What is the United Nations doing to help those countries affected by locusts? Have they been effective so far? Why or why not?

    _____

    _____

4. Compare the two feelings Aicha Bint Sadibouh has about locusts. Do you understand why he feels the way he does? Explain your answer.

    _____

    _____

    _____

5. Think of something you have always found to be beautiful or intriguing. Now imagine that very thing is also dangerous, harmful, and potentially deadly. Explain both sides of this special "thing."

    _____

    _____

    _____

6. Do poor countries have a chance to fight back without adequate resources? Before you answer, reflect on the attitudes and actions of Presidents Amadou Toumani Toure of Mali and Abdoulaye Wade of Senegal.

    _____

    _____

Attack of the Locusts (cont.)

Strength in Numbers

Some people, like Aicha Bint Sadibouth, might describe a single locust as a beautiful creature in the sky. But when it comes to a swarm of locusts, everyone agrees that they are both scary and disastrous. Use the pictures below to answer the questions.

Lifecycle of a Locust

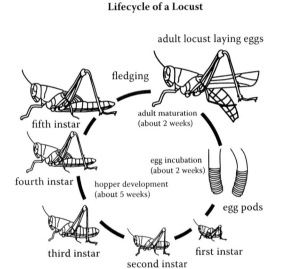

Damaged Incurred by a Swarm of Locusts

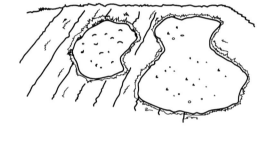

1. Look at picture 1. Does a locust appear threatening to you? Now look at picture 2. Do your feelings change after seeing what a swarm of locusts can do? Explain your feelings.

   _____

   _____

2. Imagine you are a farmer and picture 2 is your land. Think about all the various ways your life and the lives of others would be affected. Describe how this devastation would affect your family, the economy, hunger, other animals that depend on the crops, and the overall morale of the people around you.

   _____

   _____

   _____

3. Pretend you are a leader of a country that has been left with nothing after an attack from a swarm of locusts wiped everything out. Write a letter to the United Nations describing the devastation and desperate need for assistance. Think of what you need in order to keep your people safe from starvation, economic hardship, etc. Use the back of this page to write your letter.

Attack of the Locusts (cont.)

Document-Based Extension Activities

Students may work independently, or the teacher may copy this page and cut out the activities and distribute them to the students for completion in small groups.

1. Create a before-and-after illustration of a piece of land devastated by locusts.

2. Use the Internet to find the countries in the world that have been affected by locusts in the past and are likely to suffer future attacks. Then use a map of the world to highlight those areas and share them with the class.

3. Write a newspaper article, complete with photos, that reports on a recent attack by a swarm of locusts. If you prefer, pretend you are an on-scene reporter, and share your news story with the class.

4. Using a poster board or construction paper, draw the lifecycle of a locust. Then research the scientific classification of a locust to include on your illustration.

Bigfoot? Big Hoax!

In 1958, a logger in a California forest found the tracks of a giant beast: footprints 16 inches long. Newspapers across the country reported that the prints belonged to a hairy, humanlike creature they called Bigfoot. Bigfoot has lived on as a modern mystery ever since.

Then in 2002, a news flash: Bigfoot was a big fake. Michael Wallace announced that his father, Ray, had made the tracks in 1958 with a pair of wooden feet. After Ray died on November 26, his family decided to put the myth to rest. "Dad was a real character," Michael said. "He really knew how to tell a story, and the world was ready for Bigfoot."

Bigfoot believers say this recent confession doesn't mean a thing. They say they knew the story was a hoax and that it doesn't explain hundreds of other sightings, footprints, and tales. A mythical apelike creature, also known as Yeti or Sasquatch, has been part of Asian, European, and Native American folklore for centuries.

Most scientists agree that Bigfoot is nothing more than a very tall tale. Almost all of the footprints ever found have turned out to be man-made. There is no hard evidence of Bigfoot, such as bones, for scientists to study. "How could an animal exist for so long without a fossil record?" asks scientist Russell Ciochon.

For something that doesn't exist, Bigfoot surely makes tracks! Even today, reports of this creature and its prints continue to pour in. Jeff Meldrum of Idaho State University is one of the only scientists who believes Bigfoot could be real. He says that the lack of scientific proof is just one more reason to take Bigfoot seriously. "Science is about exploring the unknown," he says.

Bigfoot? Big Hoax! *(cont.)*

Directions: Answer the questions. You may use the article.

1. When was the first discovery of Bigfoot's footprints? Who found them? How big were they?

   _____

   _____

2. What other names are used for Bigfoot?

   _____

3. What cultures, other than American, have had a mythical apelike creature in their folklore history for centuries?

   _____

   _____

4. Discuss Mike Wallace's confession. What was it? When did he do it? What does his confession mean to scientists and Bigfoot believers?

   _____

   _____

   _____

5. Explain why most scientists agree that Bigfoot is nothing more than just a very tall tale.

   _____

   _____

6. Make a comparison between the beliefs shared by most scientists and the belief of scientist Jeff Meldrum on the subject of Bigfoot. With whom do you agree? Explain your answer.

   _____

   _____

7. Write a newspaper article that describes a Bigfoot sighting you had with your family on a camping trip. Your goal is to convince readers that Bigfoot does exist. You may draw a picture for your article, too. Use the back of this page to write your article.

Bigfoot? Big Hoax! *(cont.)*

Mysterious Creatures

There are a few mysterious creatures that scientists have been studying over the years. The creatures that are the most famous around the world are Bigfoot and the Loch Ness Monster, Nessie. Use the cartoon below to help you answer the following questions.

"I'll believe in you if you'll believe in me."

1. By looking at the cartoon, can you tell in what kind of habitats the two creatures live?

    _____

    _____

2. What would you do if you were standing between these two creatures? Describe your feelings and actions.

    _____

    _____

3. Does the dialogue under the cartoon support or oppose the existence of these creatures? Explain your answer.

    _____

    _____

4. Using the Internet, or books from your school library, compile some information on both the Loch Ness Monster and Bigfoot. Look for such information as geographical location, year of the first sighting, size, etc. Use the information to help you make comparisons between the two creatures. You may illustrate your findings. Write your comparisons and make your drawings on the back of this page.

Bigfoot? Big Hoax! *(cont.)*

Document-Based Extension Activities

Students may work independently, or the teacher may copy this page and cut out the activities and distribute them to the students for completion in small groups.

1. Create your own mysterious creature. Make a poster that warns people about the possible danger of this creature. You should include, but aren't limited to, the following about your creature: a name, detailed picture, location(s) of sighting(s), description of possible danger, what to do in case of an encounter, etc.

2. Research other mysterious creatures online or in the library. Pick the two you find the most intriguing. Based on information you find, create a cartoon or newspaper article similar to the one shown for Bigfoot and Nessie.

3. Write an imaginary story about an encounter or experience you had with a mysterious creature or object. **Hint:** You may make up your own, or use one or more of the following: Bigfoot, the Loch Ness Monster, or UFOs.

4. Imagine you just found bones that you think belong to Bigfoot. Write a persuasive letter to a local scientist asking him or her to look into your recent findings. The goal of this letter is to get help now! You need to convince the scientist to drop everything to come help you.

Best Friends Forever

In 1982, some friends decided to build a paradise for unwanted animals. They bought 3,000 acres in southwest Utah and named it Angel Canyon. There, they established the Best Friends Animal Sanctuary. It had a simple goal: no more homeless pets.

Best Friends is home to more than 2,000 animals at a time. Most are dogs and cats, but there are also rabbits, horses, birds, and even wild animals. Many of them will be adopted. Others will spend life at the sanctuary. The operation is funded only by donations. More than 300 people work for Best Friends. Each year, they are joined by 4,000 to 6,000 volunteers.

From Disaster to Safety

The Best Friends mission has taken the staff to unexpected places. After Hurricane Katrina hit in 2005, Best Friends rescued about 4,000 animals from the streets of New Orleans, Louisiana, and 2,000 from area shelters. Many would have been put to sleep if they had not been rescued. About 600 of the animals were returned to their owners.

During the 2006 war in Lebanon, an animal-rights group there contacted the sanctuary. Best Friends president Michael Mountain said: "It was the anniversary of Katrina, in which people had been told to evacuate and leave their pets behind. We were seeing the same thing unfold in Israel and Lebanon."

Best Friends organized an airlift of 145 cats and 149 dogs from Lebanon to Utah. A village of tents and pens was set up and nicknamed Little Lebanon. More than 500 people applied to adopt the pets. Since November, about 150 have found new homes. Best Friends also sent money to a charity in Israel that has helped thousands of abandoned pets there.

True Lifesavers

Helena Hesayne is an architect and animal lover from Lebanon. She flew to Utah to learn more about shelters and to help out. She is now back in Lebanon. "I miss the dogs, but I know they are in great hands," Hesayne says. Maggie Shaarawi also made the long trip to Utah. "It always feels good to save a life," she says.

Best Friends Forever (cont.)

Directions: Answer the questions. You may use the article.

1. What is the purpose of the Best Friends Animal Sanctuary? When was it founded and where is it located?

   _____

   _____

2. Best Friends is built on 3,000 acres of land. The animals are fed, loved, and safe. Do you think a place like this offers animals a better chance of survival? Imagine you are a rescued animal. Compare life before the sanctuary and life after being rescued.

   _____

   _____

   _____

3. Describe how Best Friends operates.

   _____

   _____

4. Every year, Best Friends has 4,000 to 6,000 volunteers. Do you think this is a big number? Discuss some of the reasons why you think volunteers work hard to help the sanctuary.

   _____

   _____

5. Do you agree or disagree with a volunteer's choice to help save abandoned, lost, and stray animals? Explain your answer. Do you think you would like to be a volunteer some day? If so, where do you want to make a difference?

   _____

   _____

   _____

6. Summarize how Best Friends helped animals in Lebanon.

   _____

   _____

Best Friends Forever (cont.)

Welcome Home

Many animals around the world are lost, abandoned, or never had a home to begin with. Where do these animals go for food, safety, and refuge? The Best Friends Animal Sanctuary is one of the few places around the world that make it their mission to find, rescue, and protect animals in need. Use the picture below to answer the questions.

1. By looking at the sign, can you predict what type of place this is? Describe what you might see on the tour.

   _____

   _____

2. Do you think a person should take the tour and gather as much information about the sanctuary as possible before adopting an animal? Explain your answer.

   _____

   _____

3. Look at the background behind the sign. Where do you think the sanctuary is located? Based on its surroundings, do you think wild animals pose a threat to the sanctuary? Discuss why this could be dangerous.

   _____

   _____

4. Should all animals be able to come to a sanctuary like this so that the shelter does not put them to sleep? Using the back of this page, write a persuasive letter to your local animal shelter asking them to call various sanctuaries prior to putting animals to sleep. Maybe your letter will be enough to convince them to explore more of the options available to the animals in need.

Best Friends Forever *(cont.)*

Document-Based Extension Activities

Students may work independently, or the teacher may copy this page and cut out the activities and distribute them to the students for completion in small groups.

1. Imagine that you are developing your own sanctuary. Create a plan for it. What types of animals will you rescue? How will you provide care for the animals? From where will your funding come? Where will it be located? Finally, create a sign for your special place.

2. Contact your local pound or animal shelter to find out if they could use any volunteer support. They may need you to help feed, bathe, walk, or play with the animals. If they need volunteers, make a sign-up sheet for your classmates. Just think, you could become a lonely pet's new best friend!

3. Think of a time you rescued an animal, or imagine that you rescued one. Write a story that shares your experience. Tell your readers what happened from the moment you found your animal until the moment it became a part of your family. If you couldn't keep it, what did you do? To whom did you give it? Include your thoughts, feelings, and experiences.

4. Contact your local pet supply store or veterinarian to see if they offer free vaccinations for rescued animals. If they do, find a local shelter or sanctuary that could benefit from their services. If the the store or veterinarian does not offer this service, see if you can persuade them to offer their services a few times a year. For example, you can ask them to help out at a pet adoption fair.

A Tremendous Trade

In 2004, the New York Yankees rocked the baseball world by trading players to get Alex Rodriguez (A-Rod), who was widely considered the game's best player. It was the first time in major league baseball history that the current most valuable player had been traded.

A-Rod was the highest-paid player in the major leagues. His contract earns him $252 million over 10 years. Many fans celebrated A-Rod's switch to New York, saying that his presence on the team would make the upcoming season more exciting. Other baseball fans say he's overpaid.

You Get What You Pay For

Some people say the league should limit players' salaries. They argue that salaries are so high that teams with smaller budgets simply cannot afford to compete with richer teams. Other people question why baseball players earn so much more than people in other professions who may struggle to make a living. For example, how is it that a baseball player can earn more than 800 times what some teachers earn in one year?

It might not seem fair, but in every profession workers earn whatever people are willing to pay them. Baseball is no exception. Teams compete to offer as much money as they can to players who are among the major league's best, like Rodriguez. Because baseball is such a popular sport, watched by ticket-buying fans at stadiums and on television by millions, a team can earn many millions of dollars each season. Teams use much of their earnings to pay their stars' salaries, because the best players attract fans to games. For example, the Yankees sold $2 million worth of tickets since A-Rod came to town.

Can Money Buy a Winner?

With big paychecks in the bank, A-Rod and his teammates are expected to catch, throw, and swing their way to success. When the World Series rolls around, it is skills, not salaries, that count.

A Tremendous Trade (cont.)

Directions: Answer the questions. You may use the article.

1. How much money will A-Rod make on his new contract? How long is his contract?

    _____

    _____

2. Compare the salaries of professional athletes to the salaries of teachers. Do you agree or disagree with the dramatic difference? Explain your answer.

    _____

    _____

3. According to this article, why are teams willing to pay such high salaries?

    _____

    _____

4. Summarize the feelings of the people who speak out against the high salaries of professional athletes.

    _____

    _____

5. Which professions do you think should receive the highest salaries? Why?

    _____

    _____

6. Do you consider celebrities (professional athletes, actors, etc.) role models for young children and teens? Should they be expected to behave appropriately and communicate a positive message to their fans, especially the children? Explain your answers.

    _____

    _____

7. Given their large salaries, should celebrities be expected to donate to charities and help their communities? Provide some examples of ways they could use their money to help and influence others. Record your response on another sheet of paper.

A Tremendous Trade (cont.)

Too Much? Too Little?

The graph below illustrates how much money Major League Baseball (MLB) teams are currently spending on their players' salaries. Use the graph to help you answer the questions below.

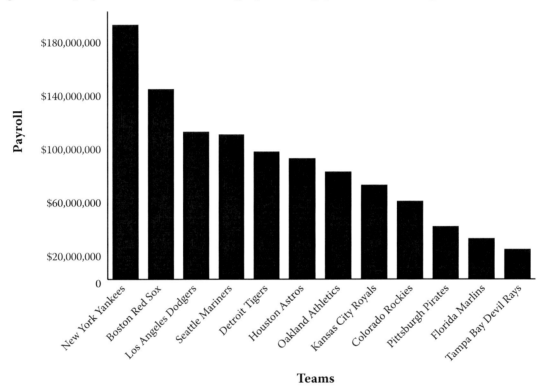

1. Which team is spending the most on players' salaries? How much are they spending? Do you think that is too much? Explain your answer.

   _____

   _____

2. Compare the payroll budgets of the New York Yankees and the Tampa Bay Devil Rays. How does the amount of money available to purchase new players affect the teams with lower budgets? Is it fair that the gaps between some teams' budgets are so dramatic?

   _____

   _____

3. Do you think the teams with higher payrolls should be held to a higher standard than other teams? If the Tampa Bay Devil Rays won the World Series, should they be respected more than if the New York Yankees won? Record your response on another sheet of paper.

A Tremendous Trade (cont.)

Document-Based Extension Activities

Students may work independently, or the teacher may copy this page and cut out the activities and distribute them to the students for completion in small groups.

1. Write a letter to your favorite celebrity or professional athlete. The purpose of your letter is to find out how this celebrity views his or her role in society. Does he or she feel that the high salary and profile come with a responsibility to their fans, communities, and to those in need? How is he or she using the money and position to make a difference?

2. Take a class poll: Should celebrities and athletes have a limit on how much money they can make? Why or why not? Share your results and responses with the class.

3. Research salaries of the following occupations: teacher, lawyer, doctor, airline pilot, dentist, computer programmer, and cook. Use a graph to illustrate the various salaries. Then, compare your results with the salaries of two athletes and two actors. Interpret your findings and share your results.

4. From where does the money come? Research how baseball teams pay these high salaries. How do they get the money? As consumers, do we help contribute to these salaries? Explain your answers.

Eight Is Enough

Poor, puny Pluto. After it was discovered in 1930, it basked in the glory of being named the ninth planet in the solar system. But in the years since, astronomers have debated whether Pluto truly is a planet. After all, it is smaller than other planets, has a strange tilt, and travels in an odd orbit. In 2006, scientists met in Prague, Czech Republic, to decide Pluto's fate. The International Astronomical Union voted on guidelines that define a planet. The result: Pluto is not a planet.

About 2,500 astronomers from 75 countries met in Prague. Some scientists proposed expanding the number of planets to 12. Pluto, its moon Charon, and two other objects, Xena and Ceres, would be planets. In the end, the astronomers decided that only Mercury, Venus, Earth, Mars, Jupiter, Saturn, Uranus, and Neptune fit the definition of "classical planets." They are celestial bodies in orbit around the sun. Their massive size allows them to be nearly round. Also, each has its own orbit. Pluto fails because its orbit overlaps Neptune's path.

All is not lost for Pluto. It has been reclassified a "dwarf planet." And that's good news for planet hunters. "Many more Plutos wait to be discovered," says Richard Binzel, a professor at the Massachusetts Institute of Technology in Cambridge.

Eight Is Enough *(cont.)*

Directions: Answer the questions. You may use the article.

1. When was Pluto discovered? What number planet was it?

   _____

2. List some of the reasons astronomers have always debated whether or not Pluto is actually a planet.

   _____

   _____

3. What group of people decided that Pluto wasn't a planet after all? Before the final decision was made, what were some scientists proposing?

   _____

   _____

4. What is the definition of a "classical planet"? Explain why Pluto doesn't fit the description. What type of planet is Pluto now?

   _____

   _____

5. Predict how this discovery will affect the future of astronomy. Will it allow scientists to be more open-minded? Will teachers teach their students about the solar system in a new way?

   _____

   _____

6. Draw a picture that depicts the dramatic change in our solar system as a result of this discovery.

7. Pretend this discovery has just been made. Compose an article for the front page of a newspaper. Your article should provide readers with a picture, an interview with a scientist, and any other relevant information. Use the back of this page to do so.

Eight Is Enough (cont.)

Goodbye, Pluto!

For years, scientists have questioned whether Pluto was a real planet. Now they finally have their answer. Pluto is no longer part of the solar system's nine planets.

1. What is the purpose of the above picture?

   _____

   _____

2. If you were new to astronomy and didn't know anything about the planets in the solar system, what could you learn from this picture? List at least five things.

   _____

   _____

   _____

3. Explain the role of an astronomer in science. Would you enjoy this type of work? Why or why not?

   _____

   _____

4. Interview your science teacher. Discuss how this recent discovery has impacted how he or she teaches students about the solar system.

   _____

   _____

Eight Is Enough (cont.)

Document-Based Extension Activities

Students may work independently, or the teacher may copy this page and cut out the activities and distribute them to the students for completion in small groups.

1. Imagine you are a cartoonist who loves to write comic strips. Create a comic strip about the loss of the ninth planet, Pluto. Your comic strip should have both pictures and dialogue. If you are unfamiliar about the features of a comic strip, read the Sunday newspaper comic section, or ask your teacher for an example.

2. Pretend you are Pluto. Write a paragraph that describes every detail about the day you found out you were no longer a planet.

3. Write a good-bye letter to Pluto from the other planets.

4. Construct two models of the solar system, one with and one without Pluto.

Too Young to Work

Valdemar Balderas was 12 when he started working in the fields. His workday began before the sun rose and ended as it set. He and his parents labored in the heat, weeding sugar beets and clearing rocks from the fields.

Valdemar, now 14, lives in Eagle Pass, Texas. He is still working in the fields. Every April, his family journeys north to begin months of grueling farmwork. Together, Valdemar and his parents earn just $500 a week for their hard work. On average, farmworkers in the United States earn less than $10,000 a year.

Forced to Work

An estimated 250 million kids are forced to work in hard and often dangerous jobs all over the world. They mine precious metals, weave rugs, and work in factories. As many as 500,000 kids in the United States and more than 100 million worldwide labor on plantations and farms.

Many countries don't have laws to protect child laborers. In the United States, a law called the Fair Labor Standards Act requires safe working conditions and limits the number of hours kids can work. But the law, which was passed in 1938, does not apply to children who toil on farms. Kids who are 12 years old are allowed to work 12-hour days in the fields with their families.

Experts estimate that more than 100,000 children and teens are injured on farms each year. They use sharp knives and scissors designed for adult hands. Many operate heavy machinery and are exposed to poisonous agricultural chemicals.

Ticket to a Better Future

Migrant families move regularly to find work in the fields. Because migrant children miss so much school, as many as 65 percent drop out. "They're so invisible," says Ellen Trevino, who works with migrants.

The Association of Farmworker Opportunity Programs is fighting to restore the money for migrant education and training programs to increase earnings for adult farmworkers. The group is also pressuring Congress to provide kids working in agriculture with the same protection as other working kids.

But for Santos Polendo and other migrant kids, education is the ticket to a better future. Polendo stopped working in the fields two years ago, after his father got sick. He will graduate from high school in May and wants to attend college and become an art teacher.

Too Young to Work (cont.)

Directions: Answer the questions. You may use the article.

1. What is the average annual salary for farmworkers in the United States? In what ways does this affect their lives?

   _____

   _____

2. List some of the dangers child farmworkers face.

   _____

   _____

3. What is a migrant? Discuss some of the problems migrant children face.

   _____

   _____

4. Describe how inconsistent school attendance may affect the children.

   _____

   _____

5. What is the Association of Farmworker Opportunity Programs doing to help migrant workers?

   _____

   _____

   _____

6. Put yourself in a child migrant worker's shoes. Do you think you would be able to handle the long days, tough working conditions, extreme heat, loss of education, and no play time? Explain your feelings.

   _____

   _____

7. Should the government be doing more to protect the children in our country? Write a letter to the president asking for action and support. Include pieces of Valdemar's sad story. Use the back of this page to write your letter.

Too Young to Work (cont.)

What Am I Missing?

For most children in the United States, education is the top priority. Children go to school every day. The goal is to get to college and get a good job. Other children go unnoticed. For these children, work is the priority, not education. Children who work in the fields miss out on being a kid and the opportunity to make better lives for themselves. Use the pictures below to compare the two different lifestyles.

1. Compare and contrast the lives of the two children in the pictures.

    _____

    _____

2. How is your life different from the pictures? How is your life similar to the pictures?

    _____

    _____

3. Explain the types of experiences the child farmworker is missing out on while he or she is away from school and friends. What lessons does a child farmworker learn in the fields?

    _____

    _____

4. Imagine your best friend is a migrant farmworker and he has to move away and get back to work. Using the back of this page, write him a letter to say good-bye. Offer support and understanding for the tough job he has ahead.

Too Young to Work (cont.)

Document-Based Extension Activities

Students may work independently, or the teacher may copy this page and cut out the activities and distribute them to the students for completion in small groups.

1. Write a paragraph that addresses the following questions: Why do some children work? What kinds of jobs do you think kids should and should not do? Who should decide when and where children are allowed to work? How would your life be different if you had to work to help support your family?

2. Write a letter to your representatives in Congress that expresses your opinions about child labor in the United States and what you think should be done about it. Convince them to change the child labor laws so that all working children are protected equally.

3. Make a poster that expresses your feelings about children working instead of getting an education. You may want to make up your own slogan and develop an action plan for fighting back and protecting all children. Share your mission with your class.

4. Write and perform a short skit about a day in the life of a child farmworker.

Green Machine

During the last few months of 2006, folks in ports throughout the United States caught a glimpse of a boat that looks as if it belongs on the set of *Star Wars*. The ship's name is *Earthrace*. The sleek silver 78-foot boat is painted with tattoo designs reflecting the crew's New Zealand heritage. On March 6, 2007, its crew was set to attempt to break a world record by circling the globe in a powerboat in less than 65 days. Along the way, they hoped to help save the planet.

Captain Pete Bethune says *Earthrace* is "the coolest-looking boat in the world." But what makes the boat even more special is the fuel that powers it. *Earthrace* runs on 100 percent biodiesel fuel. Biodiesel is an alternative to gasoline. It uses fat from animals and plants, including soybeans. Biofuel is better for the environment than regular gas because it causes less air pollution. Also, fossil fuels such as the petroleum used to make gasoline are limited resources. While working in New Zealand's oil industry, Bethune became concerned about the world's fossil fuel resources.

Earthrace has visited New Zealand and North America. "It is about connecting with people," Bethune said.

Bethune is *Earthrace's* developer and its skipper. The boat's design was inspired by a video he saw about wave-piercing hull designs. The boat cuts through the water rather than over the waves.

Bethune invites kids to visit **http://www.earthrace.net** to find out more about the race. What does he want the world to know about biofuels? "These fuels are becoming available and will work fine in cars, trucks, and buses," he says. "It's time people started using them."

Green Machine *(cont.)*

Directions: Answer the questions. You may use the article.

1. What is *Earthrace*? Describe its appearance. What are the two goals the *Earthrace* crew is planning to accomplish?

   _____

   _____

2. What is biodiesel fuel?

   _____

   _____

3. Who is Pete Bethune? Explain his role on *Earthrace*.

   _____

   _____

4. Using the description provided in the article, draw a picture of *Earthrace*. Then, write about the boat's design and the unique way it travels through water. Use the back of this page to do your work.

5. If you could meet the *Earthrace* crew, what questions would you ask?

   _____

   _____

6. Develop a final paragraph for the article that informs readers how they can help make a difference in saving the planet. Include at least five examples of how we can help protect our environment and reduce our use of limited resources.

   _____

   _____

   _____

   _____

   _____

Green Machine (cont.)

Earthrace—Start to Finish

The *Earthrace* crew has embarked on the journey of a lifetime. Study the map to get a better idea of their route and to help you answer the questions below.

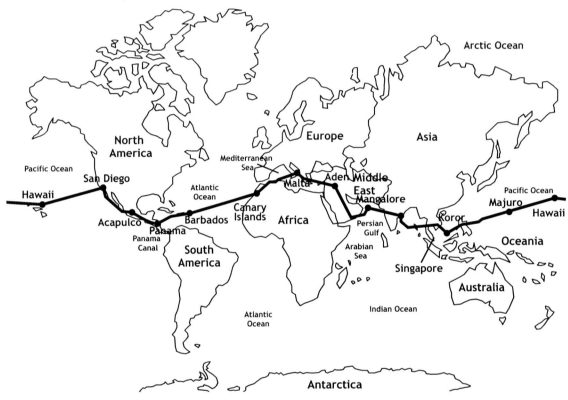

1. What is the purpose of this map?

   _____

2. List three bodies of water *Earthrace* will travel through on its journey.

   _____

   _____

3. Do you think the risks associated with the journey are worth it? Why or why not?

   _____

   _____

4. If you had the chance, would you want to be a part of the *Earthrace* crew? Explain your answer.

   _____

   _____

Green Machine *(cont.)*

Document-Based Extension Activities

Students may work independently, or the teacher may copy this page and cut out the activities and distribute them to the students for completion in small groups.

1. Write a fictional newspaper article about the experiences of the *Earthrace* crew. Imagine you were a part of the crew. What do you want people to know about your journey? Based on the goals set for your mission, were you successful? Discuss some of the following: your most exciting experience, a time when you thought of giving up, and the dangers you faced. Keep your article informative and motivating.

2. Imagine you are Captain Pete Bethune. Write five diary entries detailing your daily experiences. Be sure to include your feelings, daily routines, etc.

3. Develop your own special mission. Create an action plan using the following questions to guide you: Where would you go? How would you get there? Whom would you bring? What are the goals of your mission? You may provide any additional information you want: maps, charts, graphs, etc.

4. Construct a model of *Earthrace*. You may visit **http://www.earthrace.net** to see pictures of the boat, or use your imagination.

Feeling the Heat

Polar bears thrive in environments too harsh for most animals. For much of the year, they live and hunt on the frozen Arctic sea ice. Nature has prepared them for the harsh conditions. But nothing has prepared the bears for the danger that threatens the only home they know.

The polar bears' world is melting. Studies show that the permanent polar ice has declined by 9.8 percent every 10 years since 1978. Scientists blame global warming for the shrinking polar ice. They say that climate change is harming polar bear populations.

Recently, the United States Department of the Interior said that it was taking steps to list the polar bear as a threatened species under the Endangered Species Act. The action came on the heels of a World Conservation Union decision to move polar bears to threatened status on its Red List of Threatened Species. The World Conservation Union warns that polar bear populations could fall by 30 percent over the next 45 years.

A Bear of a Problem

Scientists estimate that 20,000 to 25,000 polar bears live in the Arctic. They are spread across five countries. Approximately 4,700 of the bears live in the United States within Alaskan waters.

Polar bears depend on the sea ice for their survival. Seals, their main prey, breed on the ice. Some melting and refreezing of the polar ice is natural. But in a warmer world, these cycles speed up, and bears have less time to hunt. Normally, they have three months in the spring when they pack on the pounds. The extra fat is used later, when the bears are not actively hunting. Pregnant females depend on this stored fat to nourish their cubs.

To Protect and Save

The Department of the Interior has a year to make its final decision. If the bears gain threatened status, the department will work with businesses and international officials to set strict rules to protect the bear and spur its recovery.

The polar bear's plight may seem distant to some. But many think that it is up to this generation to stop global warming and its dire consequences.

Feeling the Heat (cont.)

Directions: Answer the questions. You may use the article.

1. What is the purpose of this article?

   _____

   _____

2. Approximately how many polar bears live in the Arctic? How many of these bears live in the United States (within Alaskan waters)?

   _____

   _____

3. According to scientists, what is to blame for the declining permanent polar ice?

   _____

4. Summarize what is happening to the polar bears' world.

   _____

   _____

   _____

5. Scientists say that the cycle of the ice melting and refreezing is speeding up. Explain how this affects the hunting patterns of polar bears.

   _____

   _____

6. Predict what will happen to the polar bear population if we don't act now. Do you agree that it is up to current generations to stop global warming and its devastating consequences? Explain your feelings.

   _____

   _____

7. Write a persuasive letter to a government leader, such as your Congress member, convincing him or her to help you raise awareness in your community about global warming. Describe your plan to educate people about the simple steps they can take to make a big difference. Use the back of this page to write your letter.

Feeling the Heat (cont.)

Help Me!

Polar bears are used to extremely harsh conditions. However, nothing has prepared them for the effects of global warming. Global warming affects their home, daily routines, hunting patterns, population, and much more. They are depending on us to save their home. Use the picture to help you answer the questions below.

1. What is the purpose of the picture? What message is it intended to send?

   _____

   _____

2. Describe how the picture makes you feel. Does it make you want to fight back against global warming? Do you want to protect the polar bears? Explain your answers.

   _____

   _____

3. Pretend you are a polar bear. Write a story that details a typical day in your life. Describe the changes occurring around you, your fears, and the dangers you face. Use the back of this page to write your story.

4. Other than the polar bears, can you think of any other animals that are also feeling the effects of global warming? Recreate the photo above with these animals included in the picture. You can use the back of this page to make your illustration.

Feeling the Heat (cont.)

Document-Based Extension Activities

Students may work independently, or the teacher may copy this page and cut out the activities and distribute them to the students for completion in small groups.

1. Create a cartoon with pictures and dialogue that expresses your feelings on the effects of global warming on polar bears. The cartoon may be from your perspective or that of the polar bears.

2. Write a letter to the president. Your letter should be forceful and direct. You want to know why more isn't being done to protect these precious and beautiful animals. Remind the president of the devastating fate of the polar bears as a result of global warming.

3. If polar bears could speak, what do you think they would be saying to the world? Create and perform a skit about a press conference held by the polar bears. What would they say to us? Whom would they hold accountable? What questions would reporters ask them?

4. Design a graph that illustrates the polar bear population decline over time. Use the article, Internet, and other sources to help you.

Players with Pride

It is a Saturday morning in Nairobi, Kenya. Hundreds of poor kids gather at a school field in Kibera, a large slum. They play in a soccer league, and it's game day. Their equipment would surprise most United States soccer players. The kids have spades, rakes, wheelbarrows, and trash bags. They will spend five hours clearing trash, sorting items for recycling, and hauling it all away. In one year, the kids will clear more than 250 tons of garbage from their community. Digging into Kibera's mountains of trash is the only way to earn a spot on a team.

In Kibera, nearly one million people live in an area that's less than a square mile. The residents are poor, and many have health problems. There is a history of violence among members of several different ethnic groups. But an organization started by a United States Marine captain is helping Kibera's residents rise above despair and imagine a brighter future.

Hope in a Harsh Place

Rye Barcott was a student at the University of North Carolina-Chapel Hill when he first visited Kibera in 2001. He decided to start Carolina For Kibera (CFK) to help people living in the slum build richer lives. Having kids clean up Kibera before playing soccer was his idea. The league has about 2,000 kids playing on more than 200 teams, including a girls' league. Most girls in Kenya do not play organized sports.

Beyond the Soccer Field

Girls in Kibera are also rarely encouraged to get an education. Traditionally, women marry young. A CFK group called Binti Pamoja, which is Swahili for Daughters United, is helping girls to envision a new kind of life. "I see CFK's impact in their hope, vitality and dignity," says Kimberly Chapman, the chairperson of CFK's board of directors. Chapman volunteers her time for CFK in North Carolina, where she lives. She makes the 15-hour trip to Nairobi at least once each year.

With the United States Centers for Disease Control and Prevention, the group supports a free health clinic in Kibera. More than 15,000 patients per year visit the Tabitha Clinic, which has two full-time doctors and many staff members from the community.

In every program that CFK sponsors, Kiberans take responsibility and have the power to make decisions. "CFK values that nothing in life is free," says Salim Mohamed, the sports programs manager in Kenya. "Everything has to be earned. The young people have learned that they can contribute to the solutions that affect the community."

Players with Pride (cont.)

Directions: Answer the questions. You may use the article.

1. What equipment do the kids show up with on game day? Why?

   _____

   _____

2. How much garbage will the kids clear from their community each year?

   _____

3. Who is Rye Barcott? What is the name of his organization? Summarize how Barcott's organization helps Kibera's residents rise above despair and imagine a brighter future.

   _____

   _____

   _____

4. How is CFK encouraging equality between girls and boys? How are the group, Binti Pamoja, and Kimberly Chapman supporting this effort? Is this an important step? Why or why not?

   _____

   _____

   _____

5. Compare a typical soccer player's weekend in the United States with that of a child from Kibera. Do you think more children should take responsibility for themselves and their community? What about having the power to make decisions?

   _____

   _____

   _____

6. Write a paragraph about the relationship between CFK and the United States Centers for Disease Control and Prevention. Describe their efforts, growth, and accomplishments. Use the back of this page to write your paragraph.

Players with Pride (cont.)

Soccer Here, Soccer There

For many children around the world, participating in sports is a part of their everyday life. For them, playing is almost a given, not something that they have earned. For others, playing sports is an absolute privilege. They must work hard before they are given the opportunity to play hard. Use the pictures to answer the questions below.

1. What differences do you notice between the groups of soccer players?

   _____

   _____

2. Do you think fancy uniforms, proper shoes, and better fields have anything to do with whether a child has fun playing soccer? Explain your answer.

   _____

   _____

3. Write a thank-you letter to CFK's founder, Rye Barcott, for all that his organization has done to improve the soccer conditions in Kibera. Refer back to the article if necessary. Use the back of this page to write your letter.

4. Do you remember Salim Mohamed's quotes at the end of the article? Do you agree that when you work hard for something, the reward is worth much more to you than if you had simply been given it?

   _____

   _____

Players with Pride *(cont.)*

Document-Based Extension Activities

Students may work independently, or the teacher may copy this page and cut out the activities and distribute them to the students for completion in small groups.

1. Use a Venn diagram to compare and contrast a child's life in the United States with a child from Kibera.

2. Write a letter to your city's sports commissioner or parks and recreation director. Your goal is to convince him or her to make children more accountable for their community. Share how Kibera has made picking up trash just as much a part of soccer as a soccer ball.

3. Read and discuss Mohamed's quote in the last paragraph of the article. How do these words affect you?

4. Identify the goals and ideals of CFK. Create a motto or phrase that defines CFK's mission.

Amazing Mars

When NASA scientists sent two rovers to Mars, they thought the mission might last three months. "In my secret heart of hearts, I was hoping to stretch it out to six months," said Stephen Squyres, one of the scientists. More than a year later, the rovers were still going strong!

Spirit and *Opportunity* continue to roam the Red Planet and send back extremely clear pictures as well as other data. Earthlings are getting a better look at Mars than they had ever hoped.

Exploring the Red Planet

In 2004, *Spirit* touched down on Mars. *Opportunity* followed, landing on the opposite side of the planet. Both rovers got to work, digging into the soil and drilling into rocks, and sending back data about their findings. They were looking for signs of water.

As luck would have it, one rover landed inside a small crater created long ago by the impact of a meteorite. The walls of the crater gave *Opportunity* a look at ancient layers of Mars' crust. Scientists think the layers were created by a shallow lake that had periodically dried up and refilled. This information confirmed what scientists had long believed: water once flowed on Mars. Water could have nourished Martian life.

The presence of water on Mars doesn't prove that life once thrived there, but it's a promising sign that it could have. *Spirit* has uncovered soil that is more than half salt, adding to the evidence that there were oceans on the planet in the past. The rovers also have detected methane gas in the Martian air. Methane is produced by living organisms. If bacteria still live under Mars's surface, they could be releasing the gas.

Revealing More Secrets

The discoveries keep coming. The *Mars Express* orbiter found what may be huge slabs of ice from a frozen sea buried under a thick layer of dust.

Spirit has already unearthed the first meteorite found on another world. Both rovers will continue to lay bare the secrets of the Red Planet. *Spirit* recently climbed a hill, looking for new places to explore. *Opportunity* is heading south toward an area that may give scientists a look at deeper layers of rock and soil than they have seen so far.

The scientists are making the most of each Martian moment. "I have no idea how much longer (the rovers) will last," Squyres said. "So you plan for the long term—but each day you drive like there's no tomorrow."

Amazing Mars *(cont.)*

Directions: Answer the questions. You may use the article.

1. What is another name for Mars?

   _____

2. Which spacecrafts are on Mars? How long was their mission expected to last? Did the spacecrafts exceed the scientists' expectations? Why?

   _____

   _____

   _____

3. Discuss what the rovers have discovered so far about the Martian landscape and environment. Explain the significance of these discoveries to scientists' effort to prove that water and life once existed on Mars.

   _____

   _____

   _____

   _____

4. Explain the scientific significance of methane gas detected on Mars.

   _____

   _____

   _____

5. List three details about Mars you learned from reading this article. Use illustrations to bring these details to life. Use the back of this page to do your work.

6. Using information you learned from reading the article, write a haiku about Mars. **Reminder:** A haiku is a three-lined poem. The first and third lines each contain five syllables. The second line has seven syllables.

   _____

   _____

   _____

Amazing Mars (cont.)

Name the Planet!

Use the Venn diagram detailing the similarities and differences of Mars and Earth to help you complete the questions below.

Mars

It is the fourth planet from the sun.

It is located 142 million miles from the sun.

It is mostly covered by desert.

It has two moons.

A day on Mars is 24 hours and 37 minutes.

Its orbit takes 687 days to complete.

Both

They have seasons.

They have volcanoes.

Earth

It is the third planet from the sun.

It is located 93 million miles from the sun.

It is mostly covered by water.

It has one moon.

A day on Earth lasts 24 hours.

Its orbit takes 365 days to complete.

1. Which planet takes longer to orbit the sun? How much longer?

   _____

   _____

2. Think of another similarity between Earth and Mars that is not listed. Describe all the ways the two planets are similar.

   _____

   _____

   _____

3. Imagine you are up in space looking down on Earth and Mars. What would you be able to tell about the landscapes of both planets?

   _____

   _____

Amazing Mars *(cont.)*

Document-Based Extension Activities

Students may work independently, or the teacher may copy this page and cut out the activities and distribute them to the students for completion in small groups.

1. Interview an older member of your family about what they thought Mars would be like. Did they ever imagine that proof that water once flowed on Mars would be discovered? Did they ever think that life on Mars was really possible?

2. Write a story describing what you think life would be like on Mars.

3. You and your crew have just been chosen to go on the next mission to Mars. Everything will be provided for you once you land on Mars. However, your journey to Mars will take nine months. Think about what you will need for the journey. Choose carefully, because you may only bring 10 items.

4. Write and illustrate the front-page newspaper article for the day life is discovered on Mars.

A New Way Forward

Would more money and an additional 21,500 troops have given the United States the muscle needed to win the war in Iraq? President George W. Bush believed that it would. In a televised speech in January 2007, he laid out a plan for victory. The majority of additional United States troops would be sent to Baghdad, the country's capital, where they would work closely with Iraqis to improve security. The new troops would have brought the number of United States forces in Iraq to about 153,000.

Iraq is a patchwork of ethnic and religious groups. The groups, or sects, have battled each other for years. Bush acknowledged that his plan would not work without Iraqi cooperation.

Why We Invaded Iraq

The United States went to war in Iraq with the goal of removing dictator Saddam Hussein from power and destroying the weapons of mass destruction (WMDs) that were believed to be in the country. Iraq had long been suspected of having a program to create nuclear arms, and Hussein had used chemical weapons against his own people in the 1980s. Hussein was captured nine months after the invasion. He was brought to trial, and executed in December 2006. But no WMDs were ever found.

The United States spent more than $400 billion to fight the war. More than 3,000 United States troops died. Bush charged Secretary of State Condoleezza Rice with appointing a coordinator who will help with reconstruction. That was not an easy task. For generations, Iraq's Sunni Muslim minority controlled the country's wealth, education and best jobs. When Hussein, a Sunni, ruled, the members of his Baath Party held the top government jobs and ran the military and police. After Hussein's fall, many experienced Sunni workers were booted from their jobs. As a result, many government services suffered. The United States asked Iraqis to work together. As an incentive, the Iraqi government passed laws that gave all Iraqis a share of the country's oil wealth.

The President ended his speech by asking Americans for their patience and sacrifice. "In these dangerous times, the United States is blessed to have extraordinary and selfless men and women willing to step forward and defend us," said Bush. That is one thing on which all Americans agreed.

A New Way Forward *(cont.)*

Directions: Answer the questions. You may use the article.

1. Summarize the main points of President Bush's plan for victory in Iraq.

   _____

   _____

   _____

2. Explain the initial goals of the war. Who and what were the United States targeting?

   _____

   _____

   _____

3. Think about all the costs of the war in terms of life and money. What is happening to the Iraqi people? Using the back of this page, write a paragraph that both answers the questions and shares your feelings.

4. In your opinion, what is the greatest obstacle to peace in Iraq?

   _____

   _____

5. Write a letter of support and encouragement to an American soldier in Iraq. Use the back of this page to do so.

6. Predict what impact, positive or negative, the war in Iraq will have on both the American and Iraqi people.

   _____

   _____

7. How has the Iraqi government changed over the years? Compare what it was like prior to the war while under Hussein's reign, what it was like after his fall, and how it is now with all the changes and turmoil.

   _____

   _____

   _____

A New Way Forward (cont.)

Key Events in Iraq

The United States went to war with Iraq more than four years ago. The initial goal was to relieve the Iraqi people of Saddam Hussein's dictatorship and to destroy Iraq's weapons of mass destruction. Hussein had long been a target of controversy and distrust mostly because of the way he treated his own people. Although he used chemical weapons against his own people in the 1980s, no weapons of mass destruction were found. Below you will see the key events involving the removal of Hussein from power, the ensuing civil war, and the steps made toward rebuilding their government. Use the events and dates listed below to complete the questions.

December 2006	Saddam executed
May 2003	Saddam ousted
July 2004	Saddam goes to court
January 2005	first elections
February 2004	sectarian divide begins
August 2005	constitution drafted
December 2005	new elections
July 2006	civil war looms
November 2006	death penalty for Saddam
December 2003	Saddam captured
October 2005	constitution approved
March 2003	the war begins

1. Create a time line illustrating the above events in the order in which they occurred.

2. What were the five events from above that focused solely on Saddam Hussein? Create a separate time line showing the order in which these events occurred.

3. How long did it take for the constitution to be approved after it was drafted?

   _____

4. Research what happened to Saddam Hussein between May 2003 when he was ousted and December 2003 when he was captured. Where was he during that time? Compare his lifestyle as a dictator to his lifestyle in hiding. Record your response on another sheet of paper.

A New Way Forward (cont.)

Document-Based Extension Activities

Students may work independently, or the teacher may copy this page and cut out the activities and distribute them to the students for completion in small groups.

1. Write a letter to the president telling him what you think he should do about the war in Iraq. Pick one or two problems to discuss in your letter. Describe the problem(s) to the president and explain your position. Then, using facts and details, tell the president how you think he can help solve the problem(s).

2. Compose a short essay that expresses your point of view on the best course of action in Iraq. Should we send more troops, or bring them home?

3. Using the main events mentioned in the article, construct a time line that illustrates the order in which these events occurred.

4. Reflect on all the wonderful things that have already been done to show support to soldiers and their families. Think of an event or fund-raiser your class could plan to show your support. Brainstorm your ideas and decide which one your class wants to do. Then describe what you are going to do and how you are going to do it.

Reading, Writing, Rock Climbing

Class has started at Madison Junior High School. A few kids are playing a video game. Others are dancing. Some are even climbing the walls. Has their teacher lost control? No, students are taking a new PE class that lets them try in-line skating, video games, rock climbing, yoga, and more to help them develop lifelong fitness habits.

A Whole New Game

Madison's PE 4 Life Academy is a state-of-the-art fitness center. It has stationary bikes that hook up to virtual-reality racing games. It also has treadmills, kid-size weight-lifting equipment, a rock-climbing wall, and the video game *Dance Dance Revolution*. Madison's fitness center is one of four academies run by PE 4 Life, a group that promotes kids' fitness. PE 4 Life plans to open similar academies in every state.

The United States Centers for Disease Control and Prevention says that, at most, eight percent of the nation's schools have PE every day. Studies show that kids don't get enough exercise outside school either.

Many educators say that schools must help reverse this troubling trend. Nearly one in three United States schoolchildren is overweight, and one in seven kids is obese, or seriously overweight. Obesity can lead to heart disease and diabetes.

A study in the *New England Journal of Medicine* warns that, at this rate, obesity will likely shorten the average life span of today's younger generation by two to five years. This would be the first time in modern history that kids could have shorter and less healthful lives than their parents.

Playing Hard is Hard Work

A report in a pediatric medical journal shows that the new PE makes a difference. In a study of 50 overweight kids, researchers at the University of Wisconsin at Madison saw more fitness improvement in those who hiked, biked, or skied during gym class than in those who played traditional group sports.

Researchers are also studying how exercise affects learning. There is growing evidence that PE is good for kids' minds as well as their bodies. Madison's Phil Lawler says that healthy kids are better students. Sixth-grader Matthew Churik sees his point. He says that PE helps use up his energy.

"It's easier to pay attention," Matthew says.

Reading, Writing, Rock Climbing *(cont.)*

Directions: Answer the questions. You may use the article.

1. List some of the activities that are a part of the new PE class. Which one would you like to try?

   _____

   _____

2. What is PE 4 Life's goal?

   _____

   _____

3. Create a poster that illustrates what the PE 4 Life Academy fitness center at Madison Junior High School looks like. Use the back of this page to make your poster.

4. Describe the health issues that can result from obesity.

   _____

   _____

5. The new PE focuses more on the individual than on team sports. Explain how this method helps develop lifelong fitness habits. Why is this important?

   _____

   _____

6. Discuss the findings of the United States Centers for Disease Control and Prevention. How many days a week do you have PE? Do you agree or disagree that children need at least 60 minutes a day of exercise inside and outside of school combined? Why?

   _____

   _____

   _____

7. Researchers are studying how exercise affects learning. Do you think there is a connection between being physically and mentally active? Why or why not? Predict what future findings on this connection might show.

   _____

   _____

Reading, Writing, Rock Climbing (cont.)

Patterns of Obesity

The graph shows the increase in childhood and adolescent obesity from 1995 to 2000. It can also be used to compare the obesity patterns of girls and boys. Use the graph to answer the questions below.

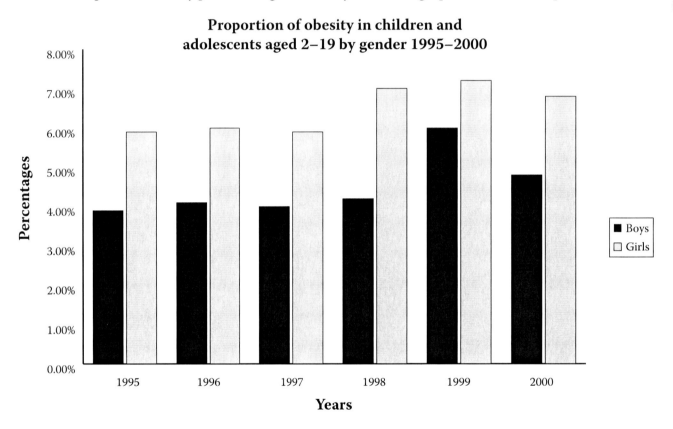

1. Compare obesity between boys and girls over the years.

   _____

   _____

2. Pretend you are a pediatrician. What advice would you give to children struggling with obesity?

   _____

   _____

3. How can children, parents, schools, teachers, and doctors work together to fight against childhood obesity?

   _____

   _____

Reading, Writing, Rock Climbing (cont.)

Document-Based Extension Activities

Students may work independently, or the teacher may copy this page and cut out the activities and distribute them to the students for completion in small groups.

1. If you could design your own physical education class, what would it look like? What lessons would you want to teach your students? In what activities would you have kids participate? How would your class encourage kids to develop healthy physical-fitness habits for life?

2. Write a letter convincing your school officials about the importance of PE class. Include such topics as obesity, lifelong fitness habits, eating right, the daily exercise recommendation for children, etc. Emphasize the amount of responsibility schools have in helping children get and stay healthy.

3. Develop a brochure about obesity. Your focus should be statistics of childhood obesity, possible health issues that result from obesity, consequences of untreated obesity, and preventing and fighting back against obesity. You may use the Internet and other sources, if necessary.

4. Keep a week-long diary of the amounts of food you eat and exercise you get each day. Provide details of what kind of food you eat, how much you eat, and the time of day you are eating (even snacks and drinks). Do the same for exercise.

Pressure at the Pump

Millions of families across the United States took car trips during the summer of 2006. Whether they went to the beach, the mountains, or Grandmother's house, one sight surely caught everyone's eye: the signs advertising high-priced gasoline. In many places in the country, the price of a gallon of gas reached a record $3 or higher.

The reason for the sky-high prices is the rising cost of oil. Crude oil is a black, sticky liquid pumped from deep beneath the earth's surface. It is one of our most important natural resources. Oil is used to heat homes and make plastics and other common materials. But most of it—some 13 million barrels a day—is turned into transportation fuel. Gasoline, diesel fuel, and jet fuel come from oil.

They Call It Black Gold

The price of this precious raw material affects anyone who goes anywhere. The airline industry must spend an extra $180 million each year for every penny increase in the price of a gallon of jet fuel. The cost of delivering any package—a birthday present, a pizza, or frozen food to a store—can go up when gas gets more expensive. Farmers spend more to fuel their tractors. Schools feel the crunch, too. They have to pay more to keep their buses running. Some are even shortening school-bus routes.

With the summer vacation season over, oil-market experts say that the price of gas should go down. But many people are already trying to beat the high price of gas by driving less, carpooling, or traveling by train or bus.

Will United States drivers decide it's smart to trade in big gas-guzzling sport-utility vehicles for gas-sipping smaller cars that get better mileage? It's probably too soon to tell. "Even if gas prices go down," says Mark Cooper of the Consumer Federation of America, "we should worry about our consumption."

"The pain at the pump is only one of the reasons that people should care," says Cooper. Burning less fossil fuel would also produce less pollution. If we cut back on driving, we will need to buy less oil from other countries. "We need to remember, " says Cooper, "that the real cost of gas is even higher than the price tag at the pump."

Pressure at the Pump (cont.)

Directions: Answer the questions. You may use the article.

1. What is crude oil? For what types of things is oil used?

   _____

   _____

2. List some of the industries most affected by the increased price of oil.

   _____

   _____

3. How much extra money must the airline industry pay each year for every penny increase in the price of a gallon of jet fuel?

   _____

   _____

4. Why do you think that gasoline prices soar so high during the summer months?

   _____

   _____

5. Discuss some of the ways we can fight the high price of gasoline.

   _____

   _____

   _____

6. Mark Cooper says that the real cost of gas is even higher than the price tag at the pump. What do you think he means? Do you agree or disagree with his position?

   _____

   _____

   _____

7. Do you think the United States should take more responsibility for pollution, consumption of nonrenewable resources, and the growing dependence we have on other countries for oil? Why or why not? Record your response on another sheet of paper.

Pressure at the Pump (cont.)

On the Road Again

Have you heard your parents complain about the high price of gas? Do they complain about how much it costs to fill up the gas tank? Do they avoid traveling long distances because it will use up too much gas? Use the cartoon to help you answer these questions.

1. What point is the artist trying to make in this cartoon?

   _____

   _____

2. How has the increase in gas prices affected your family?

   _____

   _____

3. Describe two ways that your family uses gasoline and oil.

   _____

   _____

4. Create a cartoon that represents what your family is doing to fight back against increasing oil costs. Write a paragraph discussing your cartoon and what it means. Record your response on another sheet of paper.

Pressure at the Pump (cont.)

Document-Based Extension Activities

Students may work independently, or the teacher may copy this page and cut out the activities and distribute them to the students for completion in small groups.

1. Create a skit or write a song about the different ways we use energy in our daily lives.

2. What if gasoline became too expensive for your family to purchase? Write a story detailing all the different ways your family's life would change.

3. Contact a dealership that sells hybrids, or use the Internet, to obtain as much information as you can about their hybrid vehicles. Find out how hybrids work. What makes them different from other cars on the road? What makes them better for the environment? Predict what impact driving hybrid vehicles will have on our wallets, our world, and our dependency for foreign oil.

4. Create a poster or brochure that represents three types of cars: an economy car, an SUV, and a hybrid. Compare and contrast the vehicles in the following areas: environmental emissions, safety, cost, and gas mileage. You may want to include illustrations. Then, decide which vehicle is best for you and your family.

Heart and Soles

After starting and running four businesses and losing by a sliver on TV's *Amazing Race*, Blake Mycoskie wanted to get away from it all. In January 2006, he escaped to Argentina, in South America, where he learned to sail, dance, and play polo. He also visited poor villages where few if any kids had shoes. One day, while sitting in a field on a farm, Mycoskie was inspired to do something. "I said I'm going to start a shoe company, and for every pair I sell, I'm going to give one pair to a kid in need."

So, using his own money, Mycoskie started a shoe company. He named it Toms: Shoes for Tomorrow. The company came out with its first collection of shoes for men and women last June. By the fall, Toms had sold 10,000 pairs online and in 40 stores. The shoes are priced at about $38 a pair.

Mycoskie says the slip-ons are modeled on shoes traditionally worn by Argentine workers. "I thought they had a really cool style," he says. His version of the canvas shoes goes one step further. It comes in bright colors and patterns.

Toms shoes are sold in 300 stores across the United States, and will soon be in stores in Australia, Japan, and Canada. The company will introduce a line of kids' shoes soon.

On Sole Patrol

In October of 2006, Mycoskie returned to Argentina with a couple of dozen volunteers and 10,000 pairs of Toms shoes. "I always thought I'd spend the first half of my life making money and the second half giving it away," he says. "I never thought I could do both at the same time."

Most heads of companies have the title "chief executive officer." But Mycoskie calls himself the "chief shoe giver." He plans to return to Argentina later this year to give away more shoes. He also wants to expand his shoe drops to Africa and Asia. "I believe Toms is going to give away millions of shoes one day," he says.

Heart and Soles (cont.)

Directions: Answer the questions. You may use the article.

1. What company title did Mycoskie give himself?

   _____

   _____

2. Describe what inspired Blake Mycoskie to start his shoe company. In what part of the world was he when this happened?

   _____

   _____

3. What is unique about Toms shoes? Explain the shoe company's mission.

   _____

   _____

4. Do you think your parents would be more likely to make a purchase if they knew it would support a good cause? What about you?

   _____

   _____

5. What group of people wore the shoes Mycoskie modeled his after? Describe the style of shoes. How are Toms shoes different?

   _____

   _____

6. Pretend you are one of the children living in the poor village Mycoskie visited. Compose an entry for your diary detailing the day Toms delivered free shoes to your village. Record your response on another sheet of paper.

7. What is special about Mycoskie's success? Do you think he would be as happy if he were only making money and not helping others? Why or why not? How does helping others change the way you feel inside? Discuss your feelings.

   _____

   _____

   _____

   _____

Heart and Soles (cont.)

Making the World a Better Place

Blake Mycoskie has made it his life's work to give every child in need a pair of shoes. It is people like Blake who help make our world a better place. Below, you will find a fictitious thank-you note written from the perspective of one of the young children Blake helped to live more comfortably. Use the letter to help you answer the questions.

> Dear Mr. Mycoskie,
>
> I remember the first time you came to my village for a visit. We did not have much to offer you, but we sure did have lots of fun dancing and singing with you.
>
> When you came back a few months later with shoes for all of us, I was speechless. Never before had any of us experienced such kindness. Now we can work, play, and go to school with shoes on our feet.
>
> Your generosity has improved our lives so much. I just wanted to tell you how grateful the people in my village are to you and your company. I wish you luck and look forward to hearing about all the other people around the world you are helping one pair of shoes at a time.
>
> With many thanks,
>
> Encino Cavali
>
> 10 years old

1. What is the purpose of this letter?

   _____

   _____

2. Why do you think a pair of shoes means so much to Encino?

   _____

   _____

3. How does Encino's letter make you feel? Do you think we should be more grateful for all the things we have?

   _____

   _____

4. Write a thank-you letter to someone who has gone out of his or her way to demonstrate kindness and generosity to you. Record your response on another sheet of paper.

Heart and Soles (cont.)

Document-Based Extension Activities

Students may work independently, or the teacher may copy this page and cut out the activities and distribute them to the students for completion in small groups.

1. Think of a way your class can help those in need. You can start with those around you. Maybe you can organize a food drive for local families, donate books to schools and kids who don't have enough to read, collect old clothes and donate them, collect cans and donate the money you earn to local charities, etc. These are just a few ideas to guide you, but there are so many other ways you can make a difference in someone else's life. How are you going to help change the world?

2. Find Argentina on a map or globe. What countries and bodies of water does it border?

3. Write an essay explaining what giving back means to you. Why is it important? Describe the impact giving back can have on the world.

4. Think of a way your class can help those in need. Once you have decided how you are going to make a difference, write a letter convincing your friends and community to join in. Explain your mission and how they can help you get started.

The Loss of Shuttle Columbia

History is filled with tales of brave men and women journeying into the unknown—crossing oceans, climbing mountains, and traveling to the planet's icy poles. Explorers take great risks to expand human experience and knowledge. The world was tragically reminded of those risks on February 1, 2003. Seven astronauts lost their lives as the space shuttle *Columbia* was returning to Earth after traveling six million miles through outer space. The shuttle broke apart minutes before it was to land.

The cause of the disaster is not known. Experts say that the shuttle might have overheated as it was landing. Moments before it broke apart, sensors detected high temperatures on its left side. When a shuttle reenters Earth's atmosphere, the temperature of its outer shell can reach 3,000° F. Special tiles protect it from the heat.

Three space shuttles remain in NASA's fleet. They have grown old and expensive to maintain. The shuttle was developed in the 1970s, when NASA expected space exploration to become so common and safe that scientists, teachers, and journalists would all become frequent space travelers. Some say we need a new spacecraft to replace the outdated shuttle. One possibility: small orbiter capsules like those used in early NASA missions. Although such capsules can't be reused as the shuttle can, they are smaller, safer, and cheaper.

Man vs. Machine

The *Columbia* tragedy has also sparked a debate over whether humans need to go into space at all. Some scientists believe the work that humans do in space could be done just as well by robots. A robotic aircraft has landed on Mars already and sent back valuable data.

But others believe human space travel is vital to unraveling the mysteries of our final frontier. George Faeth, a scientist at the University of Michigan, designed an experiment that was onboard *Columbia*. He believes robots can carry out some projects, but humans are essential to scientific discovery. "Just like we don't use robots to do all our work in labs on Earth, they can't do everything in space," he said.

Whichever way the program goes, most Americans believe in the value of space exploration. "Just because the mission failed doesn't mean your dreams fail," said Rachel Poppa, 17, one of dozens of students who had an experiment onboard *Columbia*. "It can be dangerous searching for answers. But you can't stop searching."

The Loss of Shuttle Columbia (cont.)

Directions: Answer the questions. You may use the article.

1. Summarize what happened on February 1, 2003.

    _____

    _____

2. How many space shuttles remain in NASA's fleet? Discuss the growing concerns about these shuttles.

    _____

    _____

3. What is an alternative for using the outdated shuttle? List the pros and cons of the shuttle and this alternative.

    _____

    _____

4. What do experts consider to be one possible cause for the disaster?

    _____

    _____

5. Compare and contrast your views and George Faeth's views on human space travel.

    _____

    _____

    _____

6. Do you think space travel should be completed by astronauts, robots, or both? Explain you answer.

    _____

    _____

7. Reread Rachel Poppa's quote in the last paragraph of the article. Do you agree or disagree with her? Explain your answer.

    _____

    _____

The Loss of Shuttle Columbia (cont.)

Historic Events in Space Exploration

Use the key events in the history of space exploration listed on the space shuttle time line to help you answer the questions below.

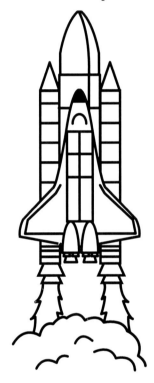

1962 United States President John F. Kennedy announces his goal of putting man on the moon before 1970.

1962 John Glenn is the first American to orbit Earth.

1969 Neil Armstrong is the first person to walk on the moon.

1975 An *Apollo* spacecraft meets and connects with a Soviet *Soyuz* craft. It is the first joint United States-Soviet mission.

1976 The unmanned *Viking I* is the first spacecraft to land on Mars.

1981 The United States space shuttle *Columbia* is launched. It is the first reusable spacecraft.

1986 The space shuttle *Challenger* explodes on its way into orbit. Seven die.

1990 Hubble, the world's first space telescope, is placed in orbit.

2000 The International Space Station receives the first crew.

2003 The space shuttle *Columbia* breaks up as it attempts to land. Seven die.

1. What was President Kennedy's goal? Did he accomplish it?

   _____

   _____

2. Who was the first person to walk on the moon? When?

   _____

3. What year did the first space shuttle tragedy take place? What was the shuttle's name?

   _____

4. How many years did it take for history to repeat itself? What was this shuttle's name?

   _____

5. The year is 1969. You are the journalist in charge of writing the front-page newspaper article about Neil Armstrong walking on the moon. Be sure to include an interview, pictures, and details of this historic event. Record your response on another sheet of paper.

The Loss of Shuttle Columbia *(cont.)*

Document-Based Extension Activities

Students may work independently, or the teacher may copy this page and cut out the activities and distribute them to the students for completion in small groups.

1. Organize a debate focusing on the question of whether to use humans or robots for space exploration. The debate should include detailed information about both options, in addition to the possibility of humans and robots working together. Include the pros and cons of each point of view.

2. Pick your favorite planet and use the Internet or other sources to learn as much as you can about its atmosphere. Then decide whether it would be best to send a robot or a team of astronauts to explore it. If you choose to send a robot, construct a model complete with a narrative description of how it will work and the purpose for its mission. If you choose to send a team of astronauts, use illustrations and mission details to answer the following questions: How will they get there? What will they need to survive? What will they wear? Choose other topics to address.

3. 10-9-8-7-6-5-4-3-2-1 blast off! You have just begun your first trip into space. Keep a diary for five days describing your daily routine, feelings, and experiences.

4. You are a TV reporter and the news just came in that the shuttle *Columbia* broke apart minutes before it was to land. Prepare your news story to share with the world. Think about the emotions you and the country are feeling, the unanswered questions, the loss of seven astronauts, etc.

The Lego® Life

Take one look around Nathan Sawaya's studio. Is there anything that this guy can't build with Lego® building blocks? Lying on the floor is a replica of Vincent Van Gogh's painting *Starry Night*. Leaning against the wall is a giant Monopoly® game board. There's even a sculpture of Curious George. All are made with Legos.

Sawaya's parents bought him his first Legos when he was three years old. Even then, he showed signs of overachievement. He popped the plastic pieces together to create a 36-square-foot city! "I'd sit there for hours," Sawaya said. "I had all these little Lego figures that I would send on adventures."

As Sawaya got older, he began to think outside the Lego box. He constructed his first portrait—a three-foot-tall image of himself—while in college. It took him two days just to build the eyes. He uses the same process to build Lego art that he used to create the portrait six years ago. First, he sketches the image onto grid paper with Lego bricks printed on it. Then, using the grid paper as a guide, he assembles the work of art with Legos.

In 2004, he quit his job as a lawyer after he won Lego's nationwide search for a master model builder. For seven months, he worked at Legoland, in Carlsbad, California, where he built a life-size T-rex. Now, he's back in New York City creating works of his own. The cost of his art ranges from $100 to tens of thousands of dollars.

Brick by brick, Sawaya has built his dreams in Legos. "I plan on never stopping," he says. "Just think how many I'll have when I grow up."

The Lego® Life (cont.)

Directions: Answer the questions. You may use the article.

1. What word(s) would you use to describe Nathan Sawaya? Why?

   _____

   _____

2. List some of Sawaya's Lego creations.

   _____

   _____

3. Describe the process Sawaya uses to build Lego art and portraits.

   _____

   _____

4. What contest did Sawaya win? Discuss how winning that competition changed his life.

   _____

   _____

5. If you could interview Nathan Sawaya, what would you want to know? Write at least four questions you would ask, and why you would ask them.

   _____

   _____

   _____

   _____

6. Reread Sawaya's quote in the last paragraph of the article. What do you think he meant by "when I grow up"?

   _____

   _____

7. Can you find inspiration in Sawaya's story? Is there something you have always dreamed of doing but didn't think you could, or should? Write a paragraph explaining your dream and what you could do to make it happen. Record your response on another sheet of paper.

The Lego® Life (cont.)

What Can You Build with Legos?

Nathan Sawaya earned the title of master model builder for Legoland in Carlsbad, California. His first assignment was to build a life-size T-rex. After seven months of hard work, his masterpiece was complete. Use the picture to answer the questions below.

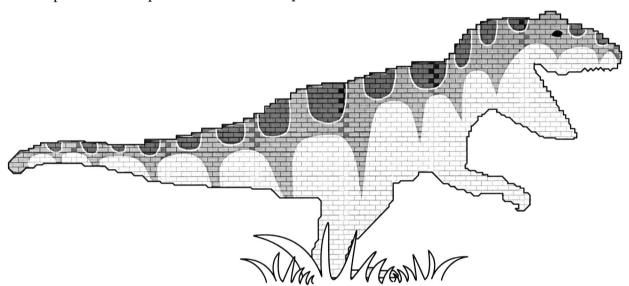

1. What does the picture tell you about Nathan Sawaya's talent?

   _____

   _____

2. If Sawaya offered to build you something, what would you choose, and why?

   _____

   _____

3. Describe what it would be like for you to watch Sawaya work.

   _____

   _____

4. Sawaya uses Legos to showcase his artistic talent. Can you name three other artists and discuss their methods of creation?

   _____

   _____

   _____

   _____

The Lego® Life (cont.)

Document-Based Extension Activities

Students may work independently, or the teacher may copy this page and cut out the activities and distribute them to the students for completion in small groups.

1. Ask your classmates to bring Legos to school. You are going to have some fun! Spend some time walking in Nathan's shoes. What would it feel like to play and build things with Legos every day? All students will participate and compete in your classroom contest. Your teacher will name winners for the categories of your choice. For example: most creativity and originality, the largest project, project with the most detail, etc.

2. Using objects of your choice, create a piece of art to share with your class. You will need to name your artwork and write a brief narrative to accompany it.

3. Pick four artists from different genres to teach your classmates about. The artists may be from the past or present, and they may be painters, sculptors, musicians, etc. You will need to share all that you know about the artist, so more research may be necessary.

4. Pick one artist you have learned about in school, or maybe one whose work you saw in a museum. Pretend you have been given the opportunity to interview the artist. What would you ask? How would you prepare for a moment like this?

Here Comes China

Liu Li has never met anyone who wears the clothes she makes. The young rice farmer's daughter works at a garment factory in the southern Chinese city of Kaiping. She stitches the seams of winter jackets that will be sold in the United States. Over the years, China has become an economic powerhouse. Chinese consumers spent some $600 billion in 2004.

Getting Down to Business

China's relationship with the United States has also changed. In 2006, China's President Hu Jintao visited the United States for the first time. He toured the offices of Microsoft, in Redmond, Washington, and met with the company's founder, Bill Gates. Later Hu visited the giant aircraft company Boeing. Then he headed to Washington, D.C., for a meeting with President George W. Bush.

At the top of the agenda was consideration of ways to ensure that trade between China and the United States benefits both countries. In 2005, China made $200 billion more on goods it sold to the United States than the United States made selling goods to China. Many of the clothes, toys, and shoes available in the United States are made in China.

Friend or Foe?

China's journey to modern life has been a long and troubled one. The country began opening up to the outside world about 150 years ago. Since 1989, China's leaders have reformed the country's economy, opening it to trade with other nations. The economies of China and the United States are more closely linked than ever. China has billions of dollars invested in the United States, making the Asian giant an important economic partner.

But China is also a business rival. United States businesses complain that Chinese companies illegally reproduce American products, including clothing, CDs, DVDs, and computer software. Chinese companies increasingly compete with American businesses for important resources such as oil, steel, and iron. Many experts expect China's drive to expand outside its borders to continue. American business leaders hope that China will compete fairly in the future.

For each country, finding common ground will require a clearer understanding of each other. For now, President Hu and President Bush promised to work together as each tries to find that common ground without giving up his nation's best interests.

Here Comes China (cont.)

Directions: Answer the questions. You may use the article.

1. Who is Liu Li, and what does she do?

   _____

   _____

2. Explain what has happened to China over the past 17 years.

   _____

   _____

3. Who is Hu Jintao?

   _____

4. When Hu traveled to the United States to meet with President Bush, what was the top priority for discussion? Why do you think this is a matter of such extreme importance?

   _____

   _____

5. Name the major United States companies officials from China have recently visited with. Explain how continued business relationships will impact both China and the United States.

   _____

   _____

6. Discuss the complaints United States businesses have for Chinese companies. Do you feel their complaints are valid? Should we be concerned? Why or why not?

   _____

   _____

7. Why is it important that both China and the United States benefit from trade?

   _____

   _____

8. Write a story about a day in the life of a child who works in a garment factory. Record your response on another sheet of paper.

Here Comes China (cont.)

Made in China

The trade relationship between China and the United States is a critical one. In order for continued economic growth, both countries must ensure fair trade practices. In 2005, China made around $200 billion more on goods sold to the United States than the United States made on selling goods to China. If you were to inspect many of the items you wear and use on a daily basis you would most likely find the words Made in China. Use the information below to help you answer the questions.

Agricultural Items

Manufactured Goods

1. What two groups of exports are shown above?

   _____

   _____

2. What agricultural items are used most in your home?

   _____

   _____

3. Were you aware that China manufactured many of the goods we use at home? Which of the manufactured items above do you use on a daily basis?

   _____

   _____

Here Comes China (cont.)

Document-Based Extension Activities

Students may work independently, or the teacher may copy this page and cut out the activities and distribute them to the students for completion in small groups.

1. Have your classmates check the tags on their clothing to determine where each item was made. Graph the results. Where were the majority of the clothing items made?

2. Draw a picture of China's flag. Conduct research to find out what each symbol on the flag represents. How long has it been the national flag of China?

3. China is a communist country and the United States is a democratic country. Research communism and democracy and write an informational essay comparing the two types of governments.

4. Find out from which countries the United States receives the most imports. List the countries in order from the highest amount of imports to the lowest amount. You may create a pie chart to help illustrate your findings.

Witness to History

When he was a kid, James Nachtwey loved to draw pictures of the Civil War and World War II. More than 40 years later, Nachtwey, a documentary photographer, is still making images of war. Now, he uses a camera.

"I'm photographing situations that need to be changed," Nachtwey, 55, said. "I think photography is a tool for social awareness. That's why I am a photographer."

Powerful images of the Vietnam War and the civil rights movement inspired Nachtwey's own work. He has covered war, famine, and critical social issues. His award-winning photographs have appeared in magazines and museums. He has been named Magazine Photographer of the Year seven times!

Nachtwey's job takes him around the world. When preparing for an assignment, he reads newspapers and magazines to research an area's issues. Once he arrives, he often uses an interpreter to speak with the local people. And he's not picky about where he stays. "A garbage bag on the ground in the jungle, or in a nice hotel, and anything in between," he says.

In December 2003, Nachtwey was injured while covering a story in Iraq for *TIME* magazine. "I'm always aware of the risk. It's part of my job," he says. Nachtwey took time off to recover, but he quickly planned his next assignment. "I use fear to help me survive, " he says. The idea is not to let fear control you, but you control the fear."

Witness to History (cont.)

Directions: Answer the questions. You may use the article.

1. How did James Nachtwey document the Civil War and World War II? Now, as a documentary photographer, what does he use to capture his images?

    _____

    _____

2. How does Nachtwey prepare for an assignment?

    _____

    _____

3. What types of situations does Nachtwey photograph? How does he view photography?

    _____

    _____

4. Would you describe Nachtwey as a successful photographer? What information from the article supports your answer?

    _____

    _____

5. Nachtwey was injured while covering a story in Iraq. Do you think the dangers he faces while on assignment are worth it? Describe how we benefit from the risks he takes.

    _____

    _____

6. Reread Nachtwey's quote at the end of the last paragraph in the article. What do you think he means? Do you agree with his point of view? Why or why not?

    _____

    _____

7. Write about a time when you were afraid to do something. Did you let the fear take over, or did you fight back against the fear? Explain your situation and how you handled it.

    _____

    _____

    _____

Witness to History (cont.)

Cameras Then and Now

The first camera was invented in 1839 by a man from France named Louis-Jacques-Mandé Daguerre. Cameras and the art of photography have come a long way since then. Use the pictures to answer the questions below.

daguerreotype   **modern camera**

1. What are the differences between the two cameras?

    _____

    _____

2. List three improvements that have been made to the camera over the years.

    _____

    _____

3. Can you think of two companies that make cameras? What type of camera do you and/or your parents use?

    _____

    _____

4. Some cell phones have cameras built into them. Explain how this feature could come in handy.

    _____

    _____

Witness to History (cont.)

Document-Based Extension Activities

Students may work independently, or the teacher may copy this page and cut out the activities and distribute them to the students for completion in small groups.

1. If you could meet James Nachtwey, what would you want to know about him and his work? List at least 10 questions you would ask him. Think about all the places he has been, things he has witnessed, his talents and awards, etc.

2. Think about what life would be like if we didn't have cameras. Write a story about how life would be different.

3. Many people put their lives at risk for our country and to help us learn more about what is going on in the world. Name two people who have been hurt, killed, or kidnapped while in Iraq. Examples include reporters, missionaries, and photographers.

4. If you could be a photographer, what would you want your focus to be? Would you want to take wedding and family photos, go around the world like Nachtwey, take scenic pictures (flowers, mountains, volcanoes, etc.), or be an underwater photographer capturing the mysteries of the sea? Explain your answer.

References Cited

Grigg, W.S., M. C. Daane, Y. Jin, and J. R. Campbell. 2003. National assessment of educational progress. The nation's report card: Reading 2002. Washington, DC: U.S. Department of Education.

Gulek, C. 2003. Preparing for high-stakes testing. *Theory Into Practice* 42 (1): 42–50.

Ivey, G. and K. Broaddus. 2000. Tailoring the fit: Reading instruction and middle school readers. *The Reading Teacher* 54 (1): 68–78.

Kletzien, S.B. 1998. Information text or narrative text? Children's preferences revisited. Paper presented at the National Reading Conference, Austin, TX.

Miller, D. 2002. *Reading with meaning: Teaching comprehension in the primary grades.* Portland, ME: Stenhouse.

Moss, B. and J. Hendershot. 2002. Exploring sixth graders' selection of nonfiction trade books. *The Reading Teacher* 56 (1): 6–18.

Pardo, L.S. 2002. Book Club for the twenty-first century. *Illinois Reading Council Journal* 30 (4): 14–23.

RAND Reading Study Group. 2002. Reading for understanding: Toward a research and development program in reading comprehension. Santa Monica, CA: Office of Education Research and Improvement.

U.S. Congress. House. 2002. *No Child Left Behind Act of 2001*, Pub. L. No. 107–110, 115 Stat. 1425.

Student Achievement Graph

Passage Title	# of Questions	Number of Questions Correctly Answered						
		1	2	3	4	5	6	7

Answer Key

Many of the answers will show an example of how the students might respond. For many of the questions there may be more than one correct answer.

Page 19

1. Fifteen-year-old Avery Hairston created RelightNY to help people who struggle to pay their energy bills by giving them compact fluorescent light bulbs, which reduce long-term energy costs and are better for the environment than regular bulbs.

2. Seventeen-year-old Kelydra Welcker invented an easy way to remove the chemical C8 from her West Virginia town's water supply. She believes everyone should be given clean and safe water to drink.

3. Answers will vary.

4. Answers will vary.

5. Answers will vary.

6. Answers will vary.

Page 20

1. Compact Fluorescent Light Bulbs (CFL) are both the most energy efficient and cost-effective over time.

2. A CFL bulb can use up to $\frac{2}{3}$ less energy and save money in the end.

3. A consumer can save $9/year by switching one bulb from an incandescent to a CFL, and $90/year by switching ten bulbs to CFLs.

Page 23

1. The Census Bureau counts the nation's population every 10 years. The last census was in 2000 and the next will be in 2010.

2. China, India, and the United States.

3. The first census was conducted in 1790 and registered 3.9 million people. The population didn't reach 100 million until 1915, and in 1967 it reached 200 million.

4. Answers may vary. Students should mention using up more than our share of the world's resources and adding more pollution into the air.

5. The population for the United States is estimated to reach 400 million by 2043. Answers will vary.

Page 23 (cont.)

6. Answers will vary.

Page 24

1. Answers will vary.

2. approximately 125 years

3. Answers will vary.

4. Answers will vary.

Page 27

1. A nebulizer is a machine that helps send medicine quickly to the lungs. It helps get a person's breathing back to normal and can potentially save his or her life.

2. Asthma attacks occur more often for elementary school-aged children in the fall between September and October. Some contributing factors are passing germs back and forth, viral infections, exercise, stress, and fall allergies such as molds and ragweed.

3. Asthma is the chronic illness that causes kids to miss the most school. Answers may vary.

4. Asthma is a chronic or long-term disease that affects a person's airways, or breathing tubes. During an asthma attack, the breathing tubes get narrower, making it harder for air to travel in and out of the lungs.

5. Answers will vary.

6. Answers will vary.

Page 28

1. The purpose of the letter is to inform schools about different ways they can work with parents, students, and doctors to reduce allergy triggers and protect students by making the school a safer place.

2. Answers will vary.

3. Answers will vary.

Page 31

1. It represents the number of Americans who die every day from the effects of smoking and secondhand smoke.

Page 31 (cont.)

2. The campaign recommends raising tobacco taxes, passing more smoke-free laws, and making sure that states spend additional money on antismoking programs.

3. Every day, about 4,000 kids try cigarettes for the first time. Answers will vary.

4. The money the states won combined with tobacco-tax earnings gave the states $21.3 billion dollars for the antitobacco fight. Of this amount, only $551 million dollars is being spent on tobacco prevention.

5. We only spend $551 million dollars on tobacco prevention, but $15.1 billion dollars is spent by the tobacco industry on advertising and sales. Answers will vary.

6. Answers will vary.

7. Answers will vary.

Page 32

1. Answers will vary.

2. Answers will vary.

3. Answers will vary.

Page 35

1. A locust starts as a wingless insect the size of a large ant. An adult locust develops wings. A single locust is harmless, but in swarms they become much more aggressive.

2. When a swarm of locusts hits, it devours every crop in sight. A swarm can destroy more than 120 miles in a single day.

3. The United Nations is coordinating efforts to help the affected countries. The goal is to spray pesticides on as many fields as possible throughout the region. The countries that have sprayed the pesticides have controlled major locust invasions. Answers will vary.

Answer Key *(cont.)*

Page 35 *(cont.)*

4. Saudibouh thinks locusts are beautiful as they fly through the sky, but when they attack he thinks they're disastrous. Answers will vary.

5. Answers will vary.

6. Answers will vary.

Page 36

1. Answers will vary.

2. Answers will vary.

3. Answers will vary.

Page 39

1. In 1958, a logger named Ray Wallace found the 16-inch footprints.

2. Bigfoot is also known by other cultures as Yeti or Sasquatch.

3. Asian, European, and Native American cultures have had an apelike creature as a part of their folklore for centuries.

4. After his dad died, Mike Wallace confessed to the world that his dad made the Bigfoot tracks with a pair of wooden feet. Answers will vary.

5. Most scientists agree that Bigfoot doesn't exist because almost all of the footprints have been man-made and no bones have been found.

6. Answers will vary, but should include that Jeff Meldrum thinks science is about exploring the unknown, so not having scientific proof is not a reason to say Bigfoot doesn't exist.

7. Answers will vary.

Page 40

1. Bigfoot lives on land. Nessie lives in water.

2. Answers will vary.

3. The cartoon is poking fun at the idea that these creatures exist. Answers will vary.

4. Answers will vary.

Page 43

1. The purpose of the sanctuary is to provide a home to homeless animals. It was founded in 1982 and is located in southwest Utah.

2. Answers will vary.

Page 43 *(cont.)*

3. Best Friends operates on donations, 300 employees, and the assistance of 4,000–6,000 volunteers each year.

4. Answers will vary.

5. Answers will vary.

6. Answers will vary, but students should mention that cats and dogs were airlifted from Lebanon to Utah.

Page 44

1. Answers will vary, but students should mention that it looks like a place for animals, and on the tour you might see where the animals sleep, eat, bathe, play, etc. The tour will help you get an idea of what goes on inside the sanctuary.

2. Answers will vary.

3. The sanctuary looks like it is in the mountains and away from the city. Answers will vary.

4. Answers will vary.

Page 47

1. A-Rod will make $252 million over 10 years.

2. A baseball player can earn more than 800 times what some teachers earn in one year. Answers will vary.

3. Teams are willing to pay high salaries because the best players attract the most fans to the games, which leads to increased ticket sales.

4. Answers will vary.

5. Answers will vary.

6. Answers will vary.

7. Answers will vary.

Page 48

1. The New York Yankees are spending nearly 200 million dollars on player salaries. Answers will vary.

2. The New York Yankees' budget is almost $200 million and the Tampa Bay Devil Rays only have just over $20 million to spend. Answers will vary.

3. Answers will vary.

Page 51

1. Pluto was discovered in 1930 and was the ninth planet in the solar system.

2. Astronomers have always debated whether or not Pluto is a planet because of its size, strange tilt, and the odd orbit in which it travels.

3. The International Astronomical Union voted that Pluto was not a planet. Scientists proposed expanding the number of planets to 12. Pluto, its moon Charon, and two other objects, Xena and Ceres, would be planets.

4. Classical planets are celestial bodies in orbit around the sun. They are massive enough to be nearly round, and each planet has its own orbit. Pluto's orbit overlaps with Neptune's path. Pluto has been reclassified as a dwarf planet.

5. Answers will vary.

6. Answers will vary.

7. Answers will vary.

Page 52

1. The purpose of the picture is to show the solar system without Pluto as the ninth planet.

2. Answers will vary.

3. Answers will vary.

4. Answers will vary.

Page 55

1. The average annual salary for farmworkers is $10,000. Answers will vary.

2. The dangers child farmworkers face are long work days in sweltering heat, operating heavy machinery, exposure to harmful chemicals, and injuries from knives and scissors made for adult hands.

3. A migrant is a person who moves regularly to find work in the fields. Migrant children miss out on school, and they risk getting sick and injured.

4. Inconsistent schooling may affect students' grades and exposure to all the curriculum; answers will vary.

Answer Key *(cont.)*

Page 55 *(cont.)*

5. The Association of Farmworker Opportunity Programs is fighting to restore the money for migrant education and training programs, and increasing earnings for adult farmworkers.

6. Answers will vary.

7. Answers will vary.

Page 56

1. Answers will vary.

2. Answers will vary.

3. Answers will vary.

4. Answers will vary.

Page 59

1. *Earthrace* is a 78-foot boat. It is sleek, silver, and painted with tattoo designs reflecting the crew's New Zealand heritage. The crew is attempting to break a world record by circling the globe in a powerboat in less than 65 days. They hope to help save the planet along the way.

2. Biodiesel fuel is an alternative to gasoline. It uses fat from animals and plants.

3. Pete Bethune developed *Earthrace* and is its skipper and captain.

4. Answers will vary.

5. Answers will vary.

6. Answers will vary.

Page 60

1. The purpose of the map is to show *Earthrace's* route.

2. Answers will vary. Answers may include Atlantic and Pacific Oceans, Panama Canal, Gulf of Mexico, etc.

3. Answers will vary.

4. Answers will vary.

Page 63

1. The purpose of the article is to inform readers about global warming and how it is affecting the polar bears. The polar bears are a threatened species.

2. Scientists estimate that between 20,000–25,000 polar bears live in the Artic. Approximately 4,700 of these bears live in the United States within Alaskan waters.

Page 63 *(cont.)*

3. Global warming is the cause for the shrinking polar ice.

4. Answers will vary.

5. Answers will vary, but students should include that the warmer it gets, the less time the polar bears have to hunt. This affects the amount of fat they store up for their inactive hunting season. Pregnant females depend on this fat to nourish their cubs.

6. Answers will vary.

7. Answers will vary.

Page 64

1. The purpose of the picture is to illustrate the point that global warming is directly affecting the polar bears. The polar bears are losing their ice.

2. Answers will vary.

3. Answers will vary.

4. Answers will vary.

Page 67

1. The kids show up with spades, rakes, wheelbarrows, and trash bags because they need to clean the community.

2. The kids clear more than 250 tons of garbage from their community each year.

3. Rye Barcott is a United States Marine captain and the founder of Carolina For Kibera (CFK). Answers may vary, but students should include that Barcott's organization helps people in the slums build richer lives and relationships that cut across ethnicity.

4. The development of a girls' league shows that the community has accepted that girls can be involved in sports, too. The group Binti Pamoja (Swahili for Daughters United), along with the group's chairperson, Kimberly Chapman, helps girls to envision a new kind of life. Answers will vary.

5. Answers will vary.

Page 67 *(cont.)*

6. Answers will vary, but the students' paragraphs should include the group's support of a free health clinic in Kibera.

Page 68

1. Answers will vary, but students should mention differences in shoes, uniforms, and playing conditions.

2. Answers will vary.

3. Answers will vary.

4. Answers will vary.

Page 71

1. Mars is also known as the Red Planet.

2. The two spacecrafts on Mars are *Spirit* and *Opportunity*. Scientists thought the mission might last three months, but they are still there! Answers will vary.

3. *Opportunity* found ancient layers of Martian crust, which they believe were created by a shallow lake that periodically dried up and refilled. *Spirit* uncovered soil that was more than half salt, adding to the evidence that there were oceans on Mars in the past. Methane gas (produced by living organisms) was also detected. The *Mars Express* orbiter found what may be ice slabs from a frozen sea buried under a thick layer of crust. *Spirit* discovered the first meteorite found on another world. Answers will vary.

4. Methane gas is produced by living organisms. If bacteria still live under Mars' surface, they could be releasing the gas. If this is truly methane gas, then some sort of life once existed on Mars.

5. Answers will vary.

6. Answers will vary.

Page 72

1. It takes Mars 322 days longer than Earth to orbit the sun.

2. Answers will vary.

3. Answers will vary.

Answer Key (cont.)

Page 75

1. Answers will vary, but should include sending 21,500 more troops to Iraq, the majority of which will be sent to Baghdad (Iraq's capital). Here they will work with the Iraqis to improve security.

2. The initial goals of the war were to remove dictator Saddam Hussein from power and destroy the weapons of mass destruction that were believed to be in the country.

3. Answers will vary.

4. Answers will vary.

5. Answers will vary.

6. Answers will vary.

7. Answers will vary.

Page 76

1. Students should have a time line with dates in the following order: March 2003—the war begins, May 2003—Saddam ousted, December 2003—Saddam captured, February 2004—Sectarian divide begins, July 2004—Saddam goes to court, January 2005—first elections, August 2005—constitution drafted, October 2005—constitution approved, December 2005—new elections, July 2006—civil war looms, November 2006—death penalty for Saddam, December 2006—Saddam executed

2. The five events in order:

    May 2003—Saddam ousted
    December 2003—Saddam captured

    July 2004—Saddam goes to court

    Nov. 2006—death penalty for Saddam

    Dec. 2006—Saddam executed

3. It took approximately three months for the constitution to be approved.

4. Answers will vary. Students should mention he was hiding underground in very poor conditions with little food and clothing. His life as a dictator was luxurious.

Page 79

1. Some of the activities you would see are video games, dancing, rock climbing, in-line skating, yoga, etc. Answers will vary.

2. PE for Life's goal is to open similar programs in every state by 2011 in order to get other local educators to visit and learn from the model programs.

3. Answers will vary.

4. Obesity can lead to heart disease and diabetes.

5. The new PE focuses more on the individual than on team sports to avoid less-athletic kids sitting on the sidelines. By working on the individual, the new PE hopes to promote lifelong fitness habits.

6. Only eight percent of United States schools have PE daily. Also, most kids don't get enough exercise at home; answers will vary.

7. Answers will vary.

Page 80

1. Answers will vary, but should include that even though obesity in both boys and girls has increased over time, obesity in girls is significantly higher than boys.

2. Answers will vary.

3. Answers will vary.

Page 83

1. Crude oil is a black, sticky liquid pumped from deep beneath the earth's surface. Oil is used for heating homes, making plastics and other common materials. However, the majority of oil is turned into transportation fuel. Gasoline, diesel fuel, and jet fuel come from oil.

2. Airlines, farmers, schools, and delivery companies are some of the industries hit hardest by the increased price of oil.

3. Airlines spend an extra $180 million dollars each year for every penny increase in the price of a gallon of jet fuel.

4. Gas prices increase in the summer months because more people are going on vacations, so the price of gas increases with the demand.

Page 83 *(cont.)*

5. We can fight back against high gas prices by driving less, carpooling, traveling by train or bus, riding a bike, walking, etc.

6. Answers will vary.

7. Answers will vary.

Page 84

1. The point the cartoon is trying to make is that gas prices are out of control.

2. Answers will vary.

3. Answers will vary.

4. Answers will vary.

Page 87

1. Blake Mycoskie titled himself Chief Shoe Giver (CSG).

2. Mycoskie was in Argentina when he noticed how many kids in the poor villages didn't have shoes on their feet.

3. What is unique about Toms shoes is that for every pair of shoes they sell, they give a pair to a kid in need.

4. Answers will vary.

5. Mycoskie modeled his shoes after the slip-ons worn by Argentine workers. Toms shoes come in bright colors and patterns.

6. Answers will vary.

7. Answers will vary.

Page 88

1. Encino wrote this letter to show gratitude for the generosity that changed his life.

2. Answers will vary.

3. Answers will vary.

4. Answers will vary.

Page 91

1. On February 1, 2003, seven astronauts lost their lives as the space shuttle *Columbia* was returning to Earth after traveling six million miles through outer space. The shuttle broke apart minutes before it was to land.

2. Three space shuttles remain in the fleet. There are concerns about how old the shuttles are and how expensive they are to maintain.

Answer Key *(cont.)*

Page 91 *(cont.)*

3. A possible alternative to the outdated shuttles is small orbiter capsules like those used in early NASA missions. Answers will vary.

4. Experts say the shuttle might have overheated as it was landing.

5. Answers will vary.

6. Answers will vary.

7. Answers will vary.

Page 92

1. President Kennedy's goal was to have a man walk on the moon before 1970. Yes, he accomplished his goal.

2. In 1969, Neil Armstrong was the first to walk on the moon.

3. In 1986, the space shuttle *Challenger* exploded on its way into orbit.

4. Approximately 17 years after the *Challenger* exploded, the space shuttle *Columbia* broke apart as it was getting ready to land.

5. Answers will vary.

Page 95

1. Answers may include dedicated, creative, talented, etc.

2. Nathan Sawaya's creations include a replica of Vincent Van Gogh's painting *Starry Night*, a giant Monopoly game board, a sculpture of Curious George, a 36-foot city, a life-size T. rex, a three-foot tall image of himself, etc.

3. Sawaya first sketches the image onto grid paper with Lego bricks printed on it. Then, using the grid paper as a guide, he assembles the work of art with Legos.

4. Sawaya won the contest for Legoland's master builder. Winning the competition allowed Sawaya to quit his job as a lawyer, complete his project at Legoland, and then return to New York where he now works for himself, creating and selling his works of art.

5. Answers will vary.

6. Answers will vary.

7. Answers will vary.

Page 96

1. Answers will vary.

2. Answers will vary.

3. Answers will vary.

4. Answers will vary.

Page 99

1. Liu Li is a young garment factory worker who sews clothing that will be shipped to the United States from China.

2. Answers will very. China has become a strong economic force.

3. Hu Jintao is China's president.

4. The top priority was to ensure fair trade that will benefit both China and the United States. Answers will vary.

5. Chinese officials have recently visited Microsoft and Boeing. Answers will vary.

6. The complaints of United States businesses are that China illegally reproduces American products and competes with the United States for limited resources (oil, steel, and iron). Answers will vary.

7. Answers will vary.

8. Answers will vary.

Page 100

1. Agricultural items and manufactured goods.

2. Answers will vary.

3. Answers will vary.

Page 103

1. Nachtwey used drawings to illustrate the Civil War and World War II. He now uses a camera to capture images of war.

2. He prepares for an assignment by reading newspapers and magazines about the area he is going to visit. Once he gets there, he speaks to the people through an interpreter.

3. He photographs war, famine, and critical social issues. He views photography as a tool for social awareness.

Page 103 *(cont.)*

4. Yes, he is a successful photographer. He has been named Magazine Photographer of the Year seven times, and his award-winning photographs have appeared in magazines and museums.

5. Answers will vary.

6. Answers will vary.

7. Answers will vary.

Page 104

1. Answers will vary, but may include the following on today's camera: more features, larger lens, more capabilities, flash, digital, memory, size, etc.

2. Answers will vary.

3. Answers will vary, but may include Kodak, Nikon, Panasonic, Minolta, Sony, etc.

4. Answers will vary, but may include for emergency use or to catch a special moment.